# A WORLD OF
# Desserts
# and
# Delicacies
## from

A Benjamin Company/Rutledge Book

Color Photographs by Walter Storck

Copyright© 1976 by Sokol & Company and
The Benjamin Company, Inc. All rights reserved.
Prepared and produced by Rutledge Books.
Published by The Benjamin Company, Inc.
    485 Madison Avenue
    New York, N.Y. 10022
Library of Congress Catalog Card Number: 76-5972
ISBN: 0-87502-049-6
Printed in the United States of America.

# Contents

## METRIC EQUIVALENTS

*Dry or Solid Ingredients:*
1 ounce = 28 grams
1 pound (16 ounces) = 454 grams

*Liquid Ingredients:*
1 teaspoon = 5 milliliters = 1/6 fluid ounce
3 teaspoons = 15 milliliters = 1 tablespoon = ½ fluid ounce
16 tablespoons = 237 milliliters = 1 cup = 8 fluid ounces
2 cups = 473 milliliters = 1 pint = 16 fluid ounces
1 fluid ounce = 30 milliliters
1 quart = .946 liter or approximately 1 liter

## WEIGHTS OF COMMON INGREDIENTS

4

Baking powder (1 teaspoon) - approximately 4.1 grams
Baking soda (1 teaspoon) - approximately 4.0 grams
Butter (1 cup) - approximately 224 grams
Crumbs, graham cracker (1 cup) - approximately 86 grams
Egg (1 medium) - approximately 41 grams
Flour, all-purpose, sifted (1 cup) - approximately 115 grams
Milk, whole or skim (1 cup) - approximately 242 grams
Oats, quick-cooking (1 cup) - approximately 72 grams
Oil, cooking (1 cup) - approximately 210 grams
Pecans or walnuts, chopped (1 cup) - approximately 118 grams
Salt (1 teaspoon) - approximately 6.0 grams
Sugar, brown (1 cup) - approximately 200 grams
Sugar, confectioners, sifted (1 cup) - approximately 95 grams
Sugar, granulated (1 cup) - approximately 200 grams
Water (1 cup) - approximately 237 grams

# Introduction

There are two worlds that meet in this new Solo cookbook—the first is the world of modern food development and testing to produce reliable, tasty products for you, the cook, and the second is the world of fine cooking, to present you with traditional international recipes that have been cherished and passed from generation to generation. We at Sokol & Company have worked in both of these worlds for more than eighty years, and *A World of Desserts and Delicacies* is an exciting result of our efforts. It is a book that we're proud to share with you, just as we are proud of all the products in the Solo line.

With the variety of Solo products and the assortment of recipes contained on these pages, you'll be able to create numerous appealing dishes. Solo fruit and nut fillings and fruit glazes blend beautifully with other ingredients to make delicious cakes, cookies, breads, pies, and desserts. Solo fillings can also be used to make sauces and glazes for meats and vegetables, pancakes and pastries, ice cream and cakes. Solo's spicy sauces and specialty products—dried mushrooms, coconut flakes, saffron, anchovy paste—add their good flavors, too, to many favorite dishes, both old and new. In a special Old-World Meals section are menus that suit any occasion, representing many national heritages whose distinctive foods have come to America's kitchens. Some of America's native culinary favorites are featured here as well—all cooked with fine Solo products for that extra special flavor.

# The Breadbasket

6

## COFFEE RING

1 8-inch ring or 10 biscuits

1 dozen toasted almonds
1 dozen maraschino cherries
1 (8-ounce) package refrigerated
 biscuits
¼ cup melted butter or margarine

⅓ cup sugar
½ (12-ounce) can SOLO Almond
 Filling
2 tablespoons light cream
 or sherry

Preheat oven to 400° F. Grease an 8-inch ring mold. Arrange almonds and cherries in bottom of mold. Cut refrigerated biscuits in half lengthwise. Dip each half in melted butter or margarine, then in sugar. Place half of the biscuits in bottom of prepared pan. Combine filling and cream or sherry, blending to make a smooth mixture. Spread over top of biscuits. Top with remaining biscuit halves. Bake 20 to 25 minutes, or until lightly browned. Let stand on wire rack about 3 minutes. Invert onto serving plate and remove pan. Serve either warm or cold. The ring can be cut when cold or the individual biscuits can be pulled off.

**Good Idea: Use half the can of filling here and the other half for Pecan-Filled Muffins on page 22. You can use either pecan, almond, or nut filling for either recipe.**

*Opposite: Quick Breads—Jewel Scones (page 8) and Coffee Ring*

## JEWEL SCONES

1 dozen scones

1¾ cups all-purpose flour
2 tablespoons sugar
1 tablespoon baking powder
1 teaspoon grated lemon peel
½ teaspoon salt
⅓ cup butter or margarine
2 eggs

½ cup light cream
1 egg white, lightly beaten
1 tablespoon sugar
1 (12-ounce) can SOLO filling, any desired fruit flavor

Preheat oven to 425° F. Combine flour, 2 tablespoons sugar, baking powder, grated lemon peel, and salt. Using a pastry blender or two knives, cut in butter or margarine until mixture has consistency of coarse crumbs. Beat eggs and cream together. Add to dry ingredients and stir until mixture is moistened. Turn out onto a lightly floured board and knead gently, about 15 strokes. Using a lightly floured rolling pin, roll dough into a circle about ¼ inch thick and 8 inches in diameter. Cut circle into quarters, then cut each quarter into 3 wedges. Place wedges, 1 inch apart, on a large ungreased baking sheet. With the thumb, make a 1-inch indentation in center of broad section of scone. Brush remaining portion of tops with egg white, then sprinkle with 1 tablespoon sugar. Fill each indentation with a scant 2 teaspoons of desired filling. Bake 12 minutes, or until light golden brown. Serve warm with butter, if desired.

8

**Good Idea: There is no need to transfer unused portions of SOLO fillings into glass containers, as the cans are lacquered. Unused portions can be refrigerated for several weeks, if covered.**


## SWEET DOUGH FOR COFFEE CAKES

2 coffee cakes

*With the people of Central Europe, the Germans, the Bohemians, the Austrians, and the Jewish homemakers, the Saturday or Sunday morning coffee cake (or kaffee kuchen) was a religiously followed type of home baking—an important food for the entire family.*

½ cup milk
⅓ cup sugar
¼ teaspoon salt
½ cup butter or margarine
½ cup warm water (105 – 115° F.)

2 packages active dry yeast
2 eggs, well beaten
½ teaspoon almond or vanilla extract
4 to 5 cups all-purpose flour

Scald milk. Stir in sugar, salt, and butter or margarine. Cool to luke-warm. Measure warm water into a large warm bowl. Sprinkle in yeast. Stir until dissolved. Stir in lukewarm milk mixture, beaten eggs, desired extract, and half the flour. Beat until smooth. Stir in enough additional flour to make a slightly stiff dough. Turn out onto a lightly floured board. Knead until smooth and elastic, about 8 minutes. Place in a greased bowl, turning to grease top of dough. Cover; let rise in a warm place, free from draft, until doubled in bulk, about 1 hour. Use this dough in either of the following sweet breads or in any recipe that you desire, using desired fillings or shapes.

**Good Idea: If you have an electric oven, a great place to let bread rise is in the oven with the oven light on. The light provides warmth and the oven itself is virtually draft free.**

### DATE FAN

1 coffee cake

| | |
|---|---|
| ½ **recipe Sweet Dough** | 1 **tablespoon sugar** |
| ½ **(12-ounce) can SOLO Date Filling** | ¼ **teaspoon cinnamon** |
| | 1 **tablespoon butter or margarine** |
| 2 **tablespoons unsifted all-purpose flour** | **Milk** |

9

Roll dough out on a lightly floured board into a 9- x 18-inch rectangle. Spread date filling on two-thirds of the length of the dough. Fold unspread dough over half of the spread dough, and both layers over remaining third of dough, making 3 layers of dough and 2 layers of filling. Seal edges. Place on greased baking sheet. Using kitchen scissors, cut 8 strips along length of rectangle to within 1 inch of opposite side. Separate strips slightly and twist so that filling shows. Cover; let rise in a warm place, free from draft, until doubled in bulk, about 1 hour. Preheat oven to 350° F. Combine flour, sugar, and cinnamon. Using a pastry blender or two knives, cut in butter or margarine until mixture resembles coarse cornmeal. Brush top of fan lightly with milk. Sprinkle flour mixture over top of coffee cake. Bake about 20 minutes, or until lightly browned. Remove from baking sheet and cool on wire rack.

## PRUNE RING

1 coffee cake

½ **recipe Sweet Dough**
½ **(12-ounce) can SOLO Prune Filling**

Punch dough down. On a lightly floured board, roll dough into a 10- x 16-inch rectangle. Spread with prune filling. Roll up from long side, jelly-roll fashion, to form a 16-inch roll. Pinch seam to seal. Form into a ring on a greased baking sheet. Using scissors, make cuts from top surface about two-thirds of the way through at 1-inch intervals. Turn one piece toward center, next toward outside of ring; continue in this fashion all the way around ring. Cover, let rise in a warm place, free from draft, until doubled in bulk, about 1 hour. Preheat oven to 350° F. Bake ring about 25 minutes, or until golden brown. Remove from baking sheet and cool on wire rack. Prune ring can be drizzled with a thin confectioners sugar glaze before serving, if desired.

## COCONUT ROLLS

2 dozen rolls

1 **recipe Sweet Dough**
4 **tablespoons butter or**
    **margarine, softened**

1 **cup SOLO Coconut Flake**
¼ **cup sugar**
½ **teaspoon mace**

Divide sweet dough in half. Roll each half out to an 8- x 12-inch rectangle. Spread each with 2 tablespoons softened butter or margarine. Combine coconut, sugar, and mace and sprinkle mixture over rectangles. Starting at 12-inch side, roll dough, jelly-roll fashion. Cut into 1-inch-thick slices. Place slices, cut side down, in buttered muffin pan cups. Cover and let rise in a warm place, free from draft, until doubled in bulk, 30 to 45 minutes. Preheat oven to 350° F. Bake 20 to 30 minutes, or until done. Remove from pans immediately.

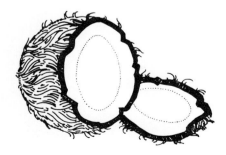

*Opposite: Yeast Breads—Prune Ring, Coconut Rolls, and Apricot-Rum Baba (page 17)*

## SWEET FREEZER DOUGH

2 coffee cakes or 2 dozen buns

| | |
|---|---|
| 5¼ to 6¼ cups all-purpose flour | 1 cup softened butter or |
| ⅓ cup sugar | margarine |
| 1 teaspoon salt | 1⅓ cups very warm water |
| ½ teaspoon grated lemon peel | (120 – 130° F.) |
| 2 packages active dry yeast | 2 eggs, at room temperature |

In large bowl of electric mixer, thoroughly combine 1½ cups flour, sugar, salt, lemon peel, and yeast. Add butter or margarine. Gradually add water. Beat at medium speed for 2 minutes, scraping bowl occasionally. Add eggs and ½ cup flour. Beat at high speed 2 minutes, scraping bowl occasionally. Stir in enough additional flour to make a soft dough. Cover and let stand 20 minutes. Turn dough out onto a well-floured board and divide in half. Shape into either of the two following variations.

## FREEZER BUNS

1 dozen buns

| | |
|---|---|
| ½ recipe Sweet Freezer Dough | Confectioners sugar |
| ½ to 1 (12-ounce) can SOLO | |
| filling, any desired flavor | |

Divide dough into 12 equal pieces. Roll each piece into an 8-inch-long strip. Twist each strip and coil into a circle, sealing ends underneath. Place on a greased baking sheet. Make wide indentations in center of each coil, pressing to bottom of dough. Spoon about 1 to 2 tablespoons desired filling into indentations. Cover loosely with plastic wrap. Freeze until firm. Remove from sheet and store in tightly closed plastic bags. Return to freezer until ready to use (these may be stored for up to 4 weeks). To bake: remove from freezer and place on ungreased baking sheet. Cover loosely with plastic wrap. Let stand at room temperature until fully thawed, about 1 hour and 45 minutes. Let rise in a warm place, free from draft, until more than doubled in bulk, about 45 minutes. Preheat oven to 375° F. Bake 15 to 20 minutes, or until evenly browned. Remove from baking sheet and cool on wire rack. Sprinkle with confectioners sugar before serving.

## FROZEN APRICOT BRAID

1 coffee cake

½ **recipe Sweet Freezer Dough**
½ **(12-ounce) can SOLO Apricot**
  **Filling**
¼ **cup all-purpose flour**

1½ **tablespoons sugar**
¼ **teaspoon cinnamon**
1½ **tablespoons butter**
  **or margarine**

Roll dough out into a 12- x 7-inch rectangle. Transfer dough to a greased baking sheet. Spread apricot filling lengthwise down center of dough. Cut 1-inch-wide strips along both sides of filling, cutting from fill-  ing out to edges of dough. Fold strips at an angle across filling, alternating from side to side. Combine flour, sugar, and cinnamon. Using a pastry blender or two knives, cut in butter or margarine until mixture is crumbly. Sprinkle mixture over top of cake. Cover with plastic wrap. Place in freezer and freeze until firm. Remove from baking sheet and wrap cake tightly in moistureproof or vaporproof freezer wrap. Return to freezer until ready to use (cake can be stored for up to 4 weeks). To bake: remove from freezer; unwrap and place on ungreased baking sheet. Cover loosely with plastic wrap. Let stand at room temperature until fully thawed, about 2 hours. Let rise in a warm place, free from draft, until more than doubled in bulk, about 1½ hours. Preheat oven to 375° F. Bake 20 to 25 minutes, or until lightly browned. Remove from baking sheet and cool on wire rack.

## HAMAN TASCHEN

15 to 18 rolls

2½ **cups all-purpose flour**
¼ **cup sugar**
1 **tablespoon baking powder**
1 **teaspoon salt**
1 **egg, well beaten**
¾ **cup milk**

⅓ **cup melted butter**
  **or margarine**
1 **(12-ounce) can SOLO**
  **Poppy Filling**
1 **egg yolk, well beaten**

Preheat oven to 350° F. Sift together flour, sugar, baking powder, and salt. Beat together egg, milk, and melted butter or margarine. Pour liquid mixture into center of flour mixture and stir until a soft dough is formed. On a lightly floured board, knead until smooth and not sticky, then roll dough out to a ¼-inch thickness. Cut into 3-inch circles. Top each circle with a small spoonful of poppy filling. Moisten edges of circle and fold three sides over the filling, leaving the filling exposed in the center and shaping the pastry into a triangle. Brush with egg yolk and place on a greased baking sheet. Bake 20 to 25 minutes, or until lightly browned. When cool, dust with confectioners sugar, if desired.

## BOHEMIAN FRUIT BUNS

3 to 4 cups all-purpose flour
¼ cup sugar
1 teaspoon salt
1 package active dry yeast
¾ cup milk
¼ cup water
¼ cup butter or margarine

1 egg, at room temperature
Oil or shortening for deep-fat frying
2 (12-ounce) cans SOLO filling, any desired fruit flavors
Confectioners sugar

In a large bowl, combine 1 cup flour, sugar, salt, and yeast. In a saucepan, combine milk, water, and butter or margarine. Heat over low heat until liquids are very warm (120 – 130° F.). (Butter or margarine need not melt entirely.) Gradually add liquids to dry ingredients and beat 2 minutes at medium speed of electric mixer, scraping bowl occasionally. Add egg and ½ cup flour. Beat at high speed 2 minutes, scraping bowl occasionally. Stir in enough additional flour to make a soft dough. Turn out onto a lightly floured board; knead until smooth and elastic, about 8 to 10 minutes. Place in a greased bowl; turn over to grease top. Cover and let rise in a warm place, free from draft, until doubled in bulk, about 1 hour. Punch dough down and turn out onto a lightly floured board. Roll dough into a ½-inch thickness. Cut with a 3-inch biscuit cutter. Place rounds on greased baking sheets. Cover and let rise in a warm place, free from draft, until doubled in bulk, about 1 hour. Heat enough oil or shortening in a large kettle to make deep fat for frying. Heat the oil to 375° F. Handling buns as little as possible to prevent their falling, fry in hot fat 2 to 3 minutes, or until brown on both sides. Drain on paper towels. When cool, make a slash in the side of each bun and fill with about1½ tablespoons desired filling. Sprinkle with confectioners sugar.

14

## SWEDISH ST. LUCIA BUNS

¾ cup milk
⅓ cup sugar
1 teaspoon salt
¼ cup butter or margarine
1 or 2 (.01-ounce) packages SOLO Saffron

1 tablespoon boiling water
½ cup warm water (105-115° F.)
2 packages active dry yeast
1 egg, well beaten
4 to 5 cups all-purpose flour
Dark seedless raisins

Scald milk in a saucepan; stir in sugar, salt, and butter or margarine. Let cool until mixture is lukewarm. Meanwhile, crush saffron with fingers and soak in boiling water; set aside. Measure warm water into a large warm bowl. Sprinkle in yeast and stir until yeast is dissolved. Add lukewarm milk mixture, egg, saffron with water, and 2 cups flour. Beat until smooth. Stir in enough additional flour to make a stiff dough. Turn out onto a lightly floured board; knead until smooth and elastic, about 8 to 10 minutes. Place in greased bowl; turn over to grease top. Cover and let rise in a warm place, free from draft, until doubled in bulk, about 1 hour. Punch dough down and let stand 10 minutes. Divide dough into 18 equal pieces. Roll each piece into a 12-inch-long strip. Cut each strip in half. Coil both ends of each 6-inch strip into center of strip. To form each bun, place two coiled strips back to back on greased baking sheets. Cover and let rise in a warm place, free from draft, until doubled in bulk, about 30 minutes. Preheat oven to 350° F. Press a raisin deep into center of each coil. Bake 15 minutes, or until done. Remove from baking sheets and cool on wire rack.

## POPPY COFFEE RING

1 9-inch ring

| | |
|---|---|
| 2 **cups all-purpose flour** | 1 **egg** |
| ½ **cup sugar** | ¾ **cup milk** |
| 3 **teaspoons baking powder** | ½ **(12-ounce) can SOLO Poppy** |
| ½ **teaspoon salt** | **Filling** |
| ⅓ **cup butter or margarine,** | 1 **teaspoon lemon juice** |
| **softened** | |

Preheat oven to 375° F. Butter a 9-inch ring mold. Sift together flour, sugar, baking powder, and salt. Using a pastry blender or two knives, cut in butter or margarine. Add egg and milk and stir just until dry ingredients are well moistened. Spoon half the batter into prepared ring mold. Combine poppy filling and lemon juice and spoon over top of dough in ring. Top with remaining dough. Bake 30 to 35 minutes, or until lightly browned. Let stand about 5 minutes, then turn out of pan onto wire rack. Serve either warm or cold.

**Good Idea: This is a delicious breakfast bread—however, it is very rich. With a special Solo topping or whipped cream, it would make an excellent dessert.**

## SOLO SWIRL COFFEE CAKE

1 coffee cake

1½ cups all-purpose flour
½ cup sugar
2 teaspoons baking powder
1 teaspoon salt
½ cup butter or margarine
2 eggs, well beaten
½ cup buttermilk

1 (12-ounce) can SOLO filling,
  any desired flavor
½ cup all-purpose flour
½ cup sugar
¼ cup butter or margarine
½ teaspoon cinnamon
½ teaspoon nutmeg

Preheat oven to 375° F. Combine flour, sugar, baking powder, and salt. Using a pastry blender or two knives, cut butter or margarine into mixture to consistency of cornmeal. Add eggs and buttermilk and stir just until dry ingredients are moistened. Spread batter into greased 9-inch-square pan. Spread filling over top and cut through filling and batter with knife, swirling filling for a marble effect. Combine remaining ingredients and sprinkle over top of cake. Bake 30 minutes, or until done.

## OATMEAL APRICOT TEA RING

1 tea ring

¼ cup warm water (105-115° F.)
1 package active dry yeast
¾ cup warm milk (105-115° F.)
¼ cup brown sugar, firmly packed
1½ teaspoons salt
4½ teaspoons butter or margarine

3½ to 4 cups all-purpose flour
½ cup quick-cooking rolled oats
½ (12-ounce) can SOLO Apricot
  Filling
1 tablespoon sugar
½ teaspoon cinnamon

Measure warm water into a large warm bowl. Sprinkle in yeast and stir until dissolved. Add warm milk, brown sugar, salt, and butter or margarine. Add 2 cups flour. Beat with rotary beater until smooth, about 1 minute. Add 1 cup flour and oats. Beat vigorously with a wooden spoon until smooth, about 150 strokes. Add enough additional flour to make a smooth dough. Turn out onto a lightly floured board and knead until smooth and elastic, about 8 to 10 minutes. Cover with plastic wrap, then a towel. Let stand 20 minutes. Roll dough out into a 10- x 16-inch rectangle. Spread with apricot filling. Sprinkle with sugar and cinnamon. Roll up from long side, jelly-roll fashion. Place on a greased baking sheet. Shape into a ring and seal ends. Using a sharp knife or scissors, cut through dough at 1½-inch intervals. Turn each cut piece over and out to form a circle. Cover, let rise in a warm place, free from draft, until doubled in bulk, about 1 hour. Preheat oven to 350° F. Bake 25 to 30 minutes, or until golden brown. Remove from baking sheet and cool on wire rack. Drizzle with confectioners sugar icing, if desired.

## APRICOT BUBBLE RING                                        1 10-inch ring

1 recipe Quick Kolacky dough  
  (see page 25)  
1 (12-ounce) can SOLO Apricot  
  Filling

½ cup melted butter or margarine  
¾ cup sugar  
1 teaspoon cinnamon

When dough has risen, punch down. Shape into balls, about 2 inches in diameter. Press a hole in the center of each ball and fill with about ½ teaspoon apricot filling. Pull dough over filling and seal tightly. Roll each ball in melted butter or margarine. Combine sugar and cinnamon and roll each ball in sugar mixture. Arrange in a well-greased 9- or 10-inch tube pan. Sprinkle dough balls with any remaining sugar mixture. Let stand in a warm place, free from draft, until doubled in bulk. Preheat oven to 350° F. Bake 35 to 40 minutes, or until lightly browned. Cool ring in pan 5 to 10 minutes. After turning it out, place it top side up on serving plate.

## APRICOT-RUM BABA                                          6 to 8 servings
*(See photo on page 10)*

¾ cup warm water (105 – 115° F.)  
1 (13¾-ounce) package hot roll  
  mix  
⅓ cup sugar  
6 tablespoons butter or margarine,  
  softened

2 eggs  
½ cup SOLO Apricot Filling  
¼ cup rum

Grease a 6½-cup baba pan. Measure water into a large warm bowl. Sprinkle yeast from roll mix over water; stir until dissolved. Add sugar, butter or margarine, and eggs and blend well. Stir in hot roll mix and beat well. Spoon batter into prepared baba pan. Cover and let rise in a warm place, free from draft, until almost doubled in bulk, 30 to 45 minutes. Preheat oven to 400° F. Bake 30 minutes. (If top of cake begins to brown too much, cover with a piece of aluminum foil.) In a small saucepan, heat apricot filling until warm. Stir in rum. Turn baba out of mold into a shallow pan. Spoon sauce over baba immediately. Continue basting with mixture until baba has absorbed all of the mixture. Cool before serving.

## SWEDISH PANCAKES

6 servings

| | |
|---|---|
| 2 eggs | 1 teaspoon salt |
| 3 cups milk | Melted butter or margarine |
| 1⅓ cups all-purpose flour | SOLO Blueberry Filling |
| 1 tablespoon sugar | Confectioners sugar |

Beat eggs and milk together. Add flour, sugar, and salt and beat until smooth. Heat swedish pancake pan slowly. Brush pan with melted butter or margarine. Stir batter, pour into depressions in pan, and bake until browned on one side. Using a small spatula, turn cakes to brown other side. Cakes should be thin, with crisp edges, and delicately browned all over. Arrange hot pancakes in a circle on a warmed plate and serve hot with blueberry filling and a sprinkling of confectioners sugar.

**Good Idea: Swedish pancake pans are now available in many housewares departments and specialty shops and are a pleasure to use. But if you don't have one, drop the batter by tablespoonfuls onto a heated griddle that has been brushed with melted butter or margarine. The shape will not be as perfect, but the taste will be equally good.**

## GERMAN PANCAKES

8 servings

| | |
|---|---|
| 6 eggs, separated | ½ teaspoon salt |
| ¼ cup all-purpose flour | SOLO filling or glaze, any |
| ¼ cup butter or margarine | desired fruit flavor |
| ¼ cup milk | Confectioners sugar |

Beat egg yolks together with flour, butter or margarine, and milk until well blended. Combine egg whites and salt and beat until stiff. Fold into yolk mixture. Melt butter or margarine in a large skillet. Pour in one-eighth of batter and cook until edges curl. Turn and brown other side. Repeat process, making seven additional pancakes. Spread each with desired filling or glaze, roll up, and sprinkle with confectioners sugar. Serve hot for dessert.

**Good Idea: Another way to prepare these pancakes is to cook them as directed until firm and then bake them in a 400° F. oven about 10 minutes, or until puffed and golden brown.**

*Opposite: Swedish Pancakes*

## PUFFY PANCAKE

2 to 4 servings

½ cup all-purpose flour
½ cup milk
2 eggs, lightly beaten
¼ cup butter or margarine

SOLO filling, any desired fruit
flavor
2 tablespoons confectioners
sugar

Preheat oven to 425° F. Combine flour, milk, and eggs and beat lightly. Batter can be lumpy. Melt butter in a 12-inch skillet with a heatproof handle. When butter is very hot, pour in batter. Bake 15 to 20 minutes, or until puffed and golden brown. Spread with filling and sprinkle with confectioners sugar. To serve, cut into wedges or roll up and cut into servings.

## PINEAPPLE-APRICOT SQUARES

1 coffee cake

3¾ to 4¼ cups all-purpose flour
1 teaspoon sugar
1 package active dry yeast
½ cup milk
½ cup water
1 cup butter or margarine

2 eggs
1 (12-ounce) can SOLO Pineapple
Filling
1 (12-ounce) can SOLO Apricot
Filling

20

In a large bowl, combine thoroughly 1¼ cups flour, sugar, and dry yeast. Combine milk, water, and butter or margarine in a saucepan. Heat over low heat until liquids are very warm (120 – 130° F.). (Butter or margarine need not melt entirely.) Gradually add to dry ingredients and beat 2 minutes at medium speed of electric mixer, scraping bowl occasionally. Add eggs and ½ cup flour. Beat at high speed 2 minutes, scraping bowl occasionally. Stir in enough additional flour to make a soft, moist dough. Divide dough in half. Pat out half the dough in the bottom of an ungreased 15- x 10- x 1-inch jelly roll pan. Combine pineapple and apricot fillings and spread over dough. Roll out remaining dough on a floured board to a shape the size of the jelly roll pan. Carefully roll dough around rolling pin, transfer to top of pan and unroll to fit over filling. Seal edges together. Snip surface of dough with scissors to allow steam to escape. Cover and let rise in a warm place, free from draft, until doubled in bulk, about 1 hour. Preheat oven to 375° F. Bake 35 to 40 minutes, or until lightly browned. Cool cake in pan. If desired, frost with confectioners sugar frosting while still warm. Cut into squares to serve.

## STRAWBERRY BRUNCH SQUARES

1¼ to 1¾ cups all-purpose flour
2 tablespoon sugar
¼ teaspoon salt
1 teaspoon grated lemon peel
1 package active dry yeast
⅓ cup milk

¼ cup water
2 tablespoons butter or margarine
1 egg, at room temperature
   Coconut Topping (recipe follows)
1 (12-ounce) can SOLO Strawberry
   Filling

In large bowl of electric mixer, combine ½ cup flour, sugar, salt, lemon peel, and dry yeast. Stir lightly. Combine milk, water, and butter or margarine in a saucepan. Heat over low heat until liquids are very warm (120 – 130° F.). (Butter or margarine need not melt entirely.) Gradually add to dry ingredients; beat mixture 2 minutes at medium speed of electric mixer, scraping bowl occasionally. Add egg and ½ cup flour. Beat at high speed 2 minutes, scraping bowl occasionally. Stir in enough additional flour to make a soft dough. Cover and let rise in a warm place, free from draft, until doubled in bulk, about 30 minutes. Stir batter down, spread in a greased 8-inch-square pan. Cover and let rise in a warm place, free from draft, until doubled in bulk, about 30 minutes. Carefully spread cooled Coconut Topping over batter. Preheat oven to 350° F. 21
Bake about 30 minutes, or until done. Remove from pan and cool on wire rack. When cool, split cake in half horizontally. Spread strawberry filling over bottom half; replace top half. Cut into squares to serve.

### Coconut Topping

⅔ cup SOLO Coconut Flake
¼ cup sugar
¼ cup butter or margarine
1 tablespoon toasted slivered
   blanched almonds

2 tablespoons honey
1 tablespoon milk
⅛ teaspoon almond extract

Combine all ingredients in a saucepan. Cook over medium heat, stirring constantly, until butter or margarine is melted and mixture is well blended. Bring to a boil and simmer 1 minute. Remove from heat and cool thoroughly before using for topping on coffee cake.

Good Idea: For a tasty variation, substitute Solo Lemon Filling for the strawberry.

## COCONUT STRAWBERRY CIRCLE

1 coffee cake

*This makes a tasty coffee cake, with just minutes of effort. It tastes equally good with almost any kind of fruit filling.*

1 (8-ounce) can refrigerated
    biscuits
¼ cup SOLO Strawberry or
    Raspberry Filling

2 tablespoons SOLO Coconut
    Flake

Preheat oven to 400° F. Butter an 8-inch layer cake pan. Separate biscuit dough into 10 biscuits. Flatten slightly and, using the back of a knife, make a crease down the center of each biscuit. Combine strawberry or raspberry filling and coconut flakes. Place about 1 heaping teaspoon of mixture in center of each biscuit and fold into half circle. Arrange folded biscuits, open side up, crosswise around outer edge of cake pan. Bake 12 to 15 minutes, or until golden brown. Cool slightly in pan before serving. Serve warm with a drizzle of confectioners sugar frosting, if desired.

22 **Good Idea: This is the coffee cake to make when you have used part of a can of filling in another recipe. You can, in fact, use several different leftover flavors, placing a different flavor in each biscuit.**

## PECAN-FILLED MUFFINS

10 muffins

1 egg, lightly beaten
½ teaspoon vanilla extract
1 tablespoon butter or margarine,
    melted
⅓ cup brown sugar, firmly
    packed

½ (11½-ounce) can SOLO Pecan
    Filling
1 (8-ounce) can refrigerated
    biscuits

Preheat oven to 375° F. Combine egg, vanilla, butter or margarine, and brown sugar and blend well. Stir in pecan filling and mix well. Separate biscuit dough into 10 biscuits and press each out slightly with the hands. Press each biscuit into a 2½-inch muffin pan cup. Press as far up the sides as possible, making the dough as thin as possible. Fill with 1 tablespoon of the pecan mixture. Bake about 15 minutes, or until lightly browned. Remove from pans and serve warm.

## DATE-FILLED BRAN MUFFINS

12 muffins

1 cup all-bran cereal
1 cup milk
1 egg
¼ cup soft butter or margarine
1 cup all-purpose flour

2½ teaspoons baking powder
½ teaspoon salt
¼ cup sugar
½ (12-ounce) can SOLO Date
   Filling

Preheat oven to 400° F. Generously butter twelve 2½-inch muffin pan cups. Combine all-bran and milk. Let stand until most of moisture is absorbed. Add egg and butter or margarine and beat well. Sift together flour, baking powder, and salt. Stir in sugar. Add to bran mixture and stir just until dry ingredients are moistened. (Batter will be lumpy.) Divide mixture among prepared muffin pan cups. Place a heaping teaspoonful of date filling in center of each muffin. Bake about 20 to 25 minutes, or until top of muffin springs back when lightly pressed with finger. Cool slightly on wire rack. Turn out of pan to cool completely.

**Good Idea: If you are making muffins of any kind and you do not have enough batter or dough to fill all of the cups, place 1 to 2 tablespoons water in the empty cups. This will keep them from burning or warping and prolong the life of the pan.**

23

## PRUNE PINWHEELS

10 rolls

3 cups all-purpose flour
4 teaspoons baking powder
½ teaspoon salt
½ cup butter or margarine,
   softened

1 cup milk
1 (12-ounce) can SOLO Prune
   Filling or any desired
   nut filling

Preheat oven to 400° F. Heavily butter a 9-inch layer cake pan. Stir together flour, baking powder, and salt. Using a pastry blender or two knives, cut in butter or margarine until mixture resembles coarse crumbs. Add milk and stir until well blended. Turn dough out onto a lightly floured board and knead 10 to 12 times, or until a smooth ball is formed. Roll dough into a 10- x 16-inch rectangle. Spread prune filling over top of dough. Starting at the long side, roll dough up, jelly-roll fashion. Moisten edge and press gently together to seal. Cut roll into 10 slices. Place slices cut side down in prepared pan. Bake 35 minutes, or until lightly browned. Serve warm. If desired, for added taste, sprinkle the bottom of the pan with brown sugar and a few nuts before rolls are placed in it.

## QUICK KOLACKY

3 to 4 dozen buns

3½ to 4½ cups all-purpose flour
3 tablespoons sugar
1 teaspoon salt
2 packages active dry yeast
1 cup milk

½ cup water
¼ cup butter or margarine
2 (12-ounce) cans SOLO filling,
any desired flavor

In a large bowl, combine 1½ cups flour, sugar, salt, and yeast. In a saucepan, combine milk, water, and butter or margarine. Heat over low heat until liquids are warm (120–130° F.). (Butter or margarine need not melt entirely.) Gradually add to dry ingredients and beat 2 minutes at medium speed of electric mixer, scraping bowl occasionally. Add ½ cup flour. Beat at high speed 2 minutes, scraping bowl occasionally. Stir in additional flour to make a soft dough. Turn out onto a lightly floured board; knead until smooth and elastic, about 5 minutes. Place in greased bowl, turning to grease top. Cover and place bowl in a pan of 98° F. water. Let rise 15 minutes. Turn dough out onto a floured board. Divide in half. Roll one half out to about a ¼-inch thickness. Cut out rounds, using a 2-inch cutter. Place rounds on a greased baking sheet. Repeat with second half of dough. Cover and let rise in a warm place, free from draft, 15 minutes. Press down center of each round with the thumb. Fill depression with desired Solo filling. Preheat oven to 425° F. Bake 12 to 14 minutes, or until lightly browned. Remove from baking sheets and cool on wire rack.

25

♪ **Good Idea: Quick Kolacky freeze beautifully and thaw rapidly to be re-warmed for Sunday morning breakfast or afternoon coffee.**

*Opposite: Quick Kolacky*

## ROSE ROLLS

3¾ to 4¼ cups all-purpose flour
½ cup sugar
2 teaspoons salt
2 packages active dry yeast
¾ cup milk

½ cup water
½ cup butter or margarine
1 egg, at room temperature
1 (12-ounce) can SOLO Cherry Filling

In a large bowl, combine 1 cup flour, sugar, salt, and yeast. In a saucepan, combine milk, water, and butter or margarine. Heat over low heat until liquids are very warm (120 − 130° F.). (Butter or margarine need not melt entirely.) Gradually add to dry ingredients and beat 2 minutes at medium speed of electric mixer, scraping bowl occasionally. Add egg and ½ cup flour. Beat at high speed 2 minutes, scraping bowl occasionally. Add enough additional flour to make a stiff batter. Cover bowl tightly with aluminum foil. Refrigerate 2 hours or overnight. Turn dough out onto a lightly floured board; divide into 18 equal pieces. Gently roll each piece into a 15-inch-long rope. Hold one end of a rope in place and wind dough around end loosely to form a coil; tuck remaining outer end firmly underneath. Repeat with each rope of dough. Place coils, about 2 inches apart, on greased baking sheets. Cover and let rise in a warm place, free from draft, until doubled in bulk, about 1 hour. Make indentations, about 1 inch wide, in center of each coil, pressing to bottom of dough. Fill indentation with cherry filling. Preheat oven to 400° F. Bake 12 to 15 minutes, or until done. Remove rolls from baking sheets and cool on wire rack. When cool, drizzle with confectioners sugar icing, if desired.

## ALMOND KRINGLE

2 coffee cakes

4 cups all-purpose flour
1 teaspoon salt
2 tablespoons sugar
1 cup butter or margarine, softened
¼ cup warm water (105 − 115° F.)
1 package active dry yeast

¾ cup milk
2 eggs, well beaten
1 (12-ounce) can SOLO Almond Filling

Browned Butter Icing
(recipe follows)

Sift together flour, salt, and sugar. Using a pastry blender or two knives, cut butter or margarine into mixture. Into a warm bowl, measure water. Sprinkle in yeast; stir until dissolved. Combine eggs and milk. Add to flour mixture along with yeast, mixing just enough to dampen flour.

Cover and refrigerate overnight. Divide dough in half. Return half to re-frigerator. On a lightly floured board, roll remaining half to an 18- x 16-inch rectangle. Spread half the almond filling in a lengthwise strip down center of dough. Fold one side over filling and overlap with other side. Pinch ends together. Turn dough over on a baking sheet so lapped side is down. Form into an oval shape. Cover dough and let rise in a warm place, free from draft, until doubled in bulk, about 1 hour. Repeat with remaining dough. Preheat oven to 375° F. Bake 25 minutes, or until golden brown. While warm, frost with Browned Butter Icing.

## Browned Butter Icing

| | |
|---|---|
| ⅓ cup butter or margarine, softened | 3 tablespoons light cream |
| | 1½ teaspoons vanilla extract |
| 3 cups sifted confectioners sugar | |

Place butter or margarine in saucepan and brown lightly over medium heat. Add sugar and blend. Stir in cream and vanilla until smooth. Use to frost Almond Kringle coffee cakes.

## BANANA NUT TEA BREAD                                    1 loaf    27

*This bread is solid and rich—almost a cake—and is excellent served at tea or coffee time.*

| | |
|---|---|
| ⅓ cup butter or margarine | 2 teaspoons baking powder |
| ⅔ cup sugar | ¼ teaspoon baking soda |
| 2 eggs | ½ teaspoon salt |
| 1 (11½-ounce) can SOLO Nut Filling | 1 cup mashed ripe bananas (2 to 3 bananas) |
| 1⅓ cups all-purpose flour | |

Preheat oven to 350° F. Thoroughly butter an 8½- x 4½-inch loaf pan. Cream butter or margarine and sugar together until fluffy. Add eggs and beat thoroughly. Add nut filling and blend until smooth. Sift together flour, baking powder, baking soda, and salt. Add to creamed mixture alternately with bananas, blending well after each addition. Turn batter into prepared pan. Bake 1 hour and 20 minutes, or until a cake tester inserted in center of bread comes out clean. Let stand in pan 5 minutes. Turn out on a wire rack and cool thoroughly before cutting.

**Good Idea: For an extra-special taste, spread loaf with a very thin layer of well-whipped cream cheese.**

## POPPY CRESCENTS

3 dozen rolls

*The women of Central Europe have known many ways to use poppy seed in their family baking or cooking. The American housewife has not the means to prepare or to grind poppy seed as has her sister in Central Europe. With Solo Poppy Filling, however, which is ground, cooked, prepared, and ready to use, a new assortment of old-world recipes is open to her.*

| | |
|---|---|
| 5¾ to 6¾ cups all-purpose flour | ¼ cup butter or margarine |
| ½ cup sugar | 2 eggs, at room temperature |
| 1½ teaspoons salt | ¼ cup melted butter or margarine |
| 2 packages active dry yeast | 1 (12-ounce) can SOLO |
| 1 cup milk | Poppy Filling |
| ⅔ cup water | |

In a large bowl, combine 1¾ cups flour, sugar, salt, and yeast. In a saucepan, combine milk, water, and butter or margarine. Heat over low heat until liquids are very warm (120 – 130° F.). (Butter or margarine need not melt entirely.) Gradually add to dry ingredients and beat 2 minutes at medium speed of electric mixer, scraping bowl occasionally. Add eggs and ½ cup flour. Beat at high speed 2 minutes, scraping bowl occasionally. Stir in enough additional flour to make a stiff dough. Turn out onto a lightly floured board; knead until smooth and elastic, about 8 to 10 times. Cover with plastic wrap, then a towel. Let stand 20 minutes. Divide dough into 3 equal pieces. Roll one piece out to a 12-inch circle. Lightly brush dough with melted butter or margarine. Cut circle into 12 pie-shaped wedges. Spoon about 2 teaspoons poppy seed filling on each wedge along the edge (opposite the point). Beginning at the outer edge, roll wedges up tightly; seal points. Place on greased baking sheet, point side down. Curve to form U-shapes. Repeat with remaining pieces of dough. Cover loosely with waxed paper brushed with oil, then cover with plastic wrap. Refrigerate 2 to 24 hours. When ready to bake, remove from refrigerator. Carefully uncover dough. Let stand at room temperature 10 minutes. Preheat oven to 400° F. Bake 12 to 15 minutes, or until done. Remove from baking sheet and cool on wire rack. Sprinkle with confectioners sugar, if desired.

## POPPY SEED BATTER BREAD

1 loaf

| | |
|---|---|
| 1¼ cups warm water (105 – 115° F.) | 2 tablespoons sugar |
| 1 package active dry yeast | 2 teaspoons salt |

| 2 tablespoons softened butter | 3 to 3⅓ cups all-purpose flour |
| or margarine | 1 egg white |
| SOLO Whole Poppy Seed | 1 tablespoon cold water |

Measure warm water into a large warm bowl. Sprinkle in yeast. Stir until dissolved. Add butter or margarine, 2 tablespoons poppy seed, sugar, and salt. Stir in 2 cups flour. Beat until well blended, about 1 minute. Stir in enough additional flour to make a soft dough. Cover; let rise in a warm place, free from draft, until doubled in bulk, about 35 minutes. Stir down. Spread dough evenly in a greased 9- x 5- x 3-inch loaf pan. Cover; let rise in a warm place, free from draft, until doubled in bulk, about 40 minutes. Preheat oven to 375° F. Combine egg white and cold water. Carefully brush on top of loaf. Sprinkle with additional poppy seed. Bake about 45 minutes, or until done. Remove from pan and cool on wire rack before slicing.

## POPPY CROWN CAKE

1 coffee cake

| 2¾ to 3¼ cups all-purpose flour | ⅓ cup milk |
| ⅓ cup sugar | 6 tablespoons butter or margarine |
| ½ teaspoon salt | 1 egg, at room temperature |
| 1 package active dry yeast | 1 (12-ounce) can SOLO Poppy |
| ⅓ cup water | Filling |

In large bowl of electric mixer, combine thoroughly 1 cup flour, sugar, salt, and yeast. Combine water, milk, and butter or margarine in a saucepan. Heat over low heat until liquids are very warm (120 − 130° F.). (Butter or margarine need not melt entirely.) Gradually add to dry ingredients and beat 2 minutes at medium speed of electric mixer, scraping bowl occasionally. Add egg and ½ cup flour. Beat at high speed 2 minutes, scraping bowl occasionally. Stir in enough additional flour to make a soft dough. Cover and let rise in a warm place, free from draft, until doubled in bulk, about 50 minutes. Turn dough out onto a lightly floured board. Knead slightly. Roll dough into a rectangle about 9 by 25 inches. Spread with poppy filling. Roll up from the long side, jelly-roll fashion. Form a circle and seal ends together. Place circle in a greased bundt pan. Cover and let rise in a warm place, free from draft, until doubled in bulk, about 1 hour. Preheat oven to 350° F. Bake 30 to 35 minutes, or until lightly browned. Let stand in pan about 3 minutes. Turn out onto a wire rack and let cool before serving. Dust with confectioners sugar, if desired.

# Old-World Meals

**ANCHOVY-STUFFED MUSHROOMS**
12 appetizers
*(See photo on page 113)*

| | |
|---|---|
| 3 tablespoons butter or margarine, melted | 1 teaspoon SOLO Anchovy Paste |
| 12 large mushroom caps | ¼ cup dairy sour cream |
| 12 thin slices white bread | Parsley sprigs |

Preheat broiler. Lightly brush melted butter or margarine on mushroom caps. Broil caps just until tender. Cut 12 rounds of bread from bread slices. Pour remaining melted butter or margarine into a skillet and fry rounds until golden brown. Combine anchovy paste and sour cream. (Add more anchovy paste for a stronger flavor, if desired.) Fill mushroom caps with mixture and place one cap on each toast round. Garnish each with a sprig of parsley.

**Good Idea: Serve these as a savory after dinner or as an hors d'oeuvre. To serve warm, place toast rounds with mushroom caps on top under the broiler for a few minutes.**

## ANCHOVY TURNOVERS

*(See photo on page 113)*

about 5½ dozen appetizers

| | |
|---|---|
| 1 cup all-purpose flour | ½ cup butter or margarine |
| 1 (3-ounce) package cream cheese, softened | 1 tube SOLO Anchovy Paste |

Combine flour, cream cheese, and butter or margarine and blend well. Shape into a ball and refrigerate at least 2 hours, or until dough is cold enough to handle. On a lightly floured board, roll dough out, a small amount at a time, to a ⅛-inch thickness. Cut into 2-inch rounds. Put about ¼ teaspoon anchovy paste in center of each round. Moisten edges of rounds and fold over to form a half-circle. Seal edges with tines of a fork and prick tops to allow steam to escape. Place on baking sheet and refrigerate until serving time. Preheat oven to 375° F. Bake 10 minutes, or until lightly browned. Serve immediately.

## OLD-FASHIONED MUSHROOM SOUP

8 servings

| | |
|---|---|
| 2 (5/16-ounce) packages SOLO Dried Mushrooms | 3 tablespoons tomato paste |
| | ¼ teaspoon salt |
| 4 tablespoons butter or margarine | ⅛ teaspoon pepper |
| 2 cups finely chopped carrots | 4 sprigs parsley |
| 2 cups finely chopped celery | Celery leaves |
| 1 cup finely chopped onions | 1 bay leaf |
| 1 clove garlic, finely minced | 2 tablespoons butter or margarine |
| 2 (10½-ounce) cans condensed beef broth | 3 tablespoons dry sherry |
| | Dairy sour cream |

Reconstitute mushrooms according to package directions. Drain, reserving liquid. Pat dry and finely chop half the mushrooms; slice remaining half and set aside. In a large saucepan, melt 4 tablespoons butter or margarine. Add chopped mushrooms and sauté 5 minutes. Add carrots, celery, onions, and garlic and sauté 5 minutes longer (add more butter or margarine if necessary). Combine broth, reserved mushroom liquid, and enough water to make 4 cups. Add to vegetables together with tomato paste, salt, and pepper. Tie parsley, celery leaves, and bay leaf together; add to saucepan. Bring to a boil. Cover; reduce heat and simmer 1 hour. Remove parsley, celery leaves, and bay leaf and discard. Purée soup in blender or food mill. Return to saucepan. In a medium skillet, melt 2 tablespoons butter or margarine. Add reserved sliced mushrooms and sauté 5 minutes. Add to soup along with sherry. Reheat. Serve with a dollop of sour cream.

## STUFFED TORTILLAS

6 servings

| | |
|---|---|
| 1 **pound lean ground beef** | **Cooking oil** |
| ½ **cup chopped onion** | 12 **tortillas** |
| 1 **tablespoon butter or margarine** | **Grated monterey jack cheese** |
| 1 **(8½-ounce) jar SOLO Taco Sauce** | **Shredded lettuce** |

Melt butter or margarine in a skillet. Add ground beef and onions and sauté until meat is cooked and onions are limp. Add taco sauce and heat thoroughly. Heat a small amount of cooking oil in another skillet. When oil is hot, dip tortillas in it quickly, only long enough to make them limp. Place them into a napkin-lined basket to keep them hot. Place cheese and lettuce in separate dishes. Divide meat mixture among warm tortillas; sprinkle cheese and lettuce on each and fold up. Eat in the hand or from a plate, using a fork.

**Good Idea: For added flavor, try sprinkling a small amount of chopped green onions on top of the tortillas.**

33

## EMPANADAS

about 5½ dozen cookies

Follow recipe for Anchovy Turnovers on page 31, substituting Solo Nut Filling for the Solo Anchovy Paste as filling. When baked, cool cookies on wire rack, then dust with confectioners sugar.

*Opposite: Stuffed Tortillas and Empanadas*

## APRICOT-ORANGE GLAZED CHICKEN

4 servings

½ orange, thinly sliced
2 tablespoons dry white wine
2 tablespoons lemon juice
2 tablespoons brown sugar
½ teaspoon salt

½ (12-ounce) can SOLO Apricot
   Filling
1 broiler-fryer chicken,
   quartered

Preheat oven to 400° F. Combine orange slices, wine, lemon juice, brown sugar, salt, and apricot filling. Blend well. Place chicken in a shallow baking pan, skin side down. Pour half the fruit mixture over chicken. Bake 20 minutes. Turn chicken pieces over and top with remaining sauce. Bake 20 minutes longer, basting occasionally, or until chicken is tender. Garnish with additional orange slices, if desired.

## FRUIT COBBLER

6 servings

1 (12-ounce) can SOLO Blueberry
   Filling
1 (12-ounce) can SOLO Pineapple
   Filling

¼ cup water
1 cup biscuit mix

Preheat oven to 425° F. Spoon blueberry filling into a 1-quart casserole or small baking dish. Dot top with spoonfuls of pineapple filling; *do not* blend. Add water to biscuit mix and stir just until blended. Drop 6 mounds of biscuit mix on top of fillings. Bake about 15 minutes, or until biscuits are lightly browned and fruit is hot and bubbly. Serve warm with heavy pouring cream or ice cream, if desired.

♫ **Good Idea: When fresh fruit is in season, combine blueberry filling with 1 to 1½ cups fresh blueberries and omit pineapple filling.**

*Opposite: Apricot-Orange Glazed Chicken and Fruit Cobbler*

## MRS. COWDEN'S HAM LOAF WITH CHERRY SAUCE

6 to 8 servings

1½ pounds ground ham
1 pound ground fresh pork
2 eggs, lightly beaten
1 cup wheat flakes
2 tablespoons chopped green pepper
2 tablespoons chopped onion

½ cup milk
1 (12-ounce) can SOLO Cherry Filling
1 tablespoon prepared mustard
¼ teaspoon ground cloves
⅛ teaspoon allspice
¼ cup cherry liqueur

Preheat oven to 350° F. Combine ground ham and pork in a mixing bowl and blend well. Add eggs, wheat flakes, green pepper, onion, and milk; blend well. Pat mixture into a 9½- x 5½- x 3-inch loaf pan. Combine cherry filling, mustard, cloves, and allspice. Spread ¼ cup of this mixture over the top of the meat. Bake 1 hour and 30 minutes. Remove from oven and let loaf cool. Drain off excess fat. Refrigerate loaf until well chilled. At serving time, combine cherry liqueur with remaining cherry mixture and heat, but do not boil. Serve hot sauce with very cold slices of ham loaf.

## STUFFED HAM SLICES

6 servings

¼ cup butter or margarine
¼ cup chopped celery
2 tablespoons snipped parsley
1 (12-ounce) can SOLO Pineapple Filling

4 cups dry bread cubes
½ teaspoon marjoram
2 slices ham (about ½ inch thick)
1½ teaspoons lemon juice

Preheat oven to 325° F. In a skillet, melt butter or margarine. Add celery and parsley and sauté until soft but not browned. Remove from heat. Stir in ¾ cup pineapple filling, bread cubes, and marjoram and blend well. Place one ham slice in a 9-inch-square baking dish. Spoon mixture over top. Top with second ham slice. Combine remaining pineapple filling and lemon juice. Spread over top of ham slices. Bake 45 minutes to 1 hour, or until piping hot and lightly browned.

## FRUITED POT ROAST

about 8 servings

2 tablespoons butter or margarine
1 3- to 4-pound bottom round roast
2 onions, sliced
1½ teaspoons salt

½ cup vinegar
2 cups water
1 (10-ounce) jar SOLO Raisin Sauce

Melt butter or margarine in heavy kettle or dutch oven. Add roast and brown on all sides. Add onions and brown lightly. Add salt, vinegar, water, and raisin sauce. Cover and simmer 2½ to 3 hours, or until meat is tender. Turn meat occasionally and, if needed, add more water to sauce. Remove roast from sauce. Slice meat and serve with hot cooked noodles or rice, if desired, and the sauce.

🎵 **Good Idea: Be sure to check the roast frequently and add water, when needed, to the sauce so that it will not stick to the kettle and burn.**

## TAMALE PIE                                                        8 servings

| | |
|---|---|
| 5 tablespoons cooking oil | 1 (12-ounce) can whole kernel corn |
| 2 onions, thinly sliced | ½ cup chopped green pepper |
| 3 cloves garlic, minced | 2 teaspoons salt |
| 1½ pounds ground beef | 4½ cups boiling water |
| 1½ teaspoons salt | 1½ cups yellow cornmeal |
| 2 tablespoons chili powder | ½ cup grated mild cheddar cheese |
| 2 (8½-ounce) jars SOLO Taco Sauce | |
| 1½ cups sliced pitted ripe olives | |

Heat oil in a large skillet. Add onion slices and brown lightly. Remove onions. Add garlic and ground beef and cook, stirring, until lightly browned. Add 1½ teaspoons salt, chili powder, taco sauce, olives, corn, green pepper, and cooked onions. Cover and simmer while cooking cornmeal. Add 2 teaspoons salt to boiling water. Add cornmeal slowly, stirring constantly while pouring. Cook over low heat 15 minutes, stirring occasionally. Preheat oven to 375° F. Line an oiled 9-inch casserole with a layer of cornmeal mush. Pour meat mixture carefully over the cornmeal. Cover with remaining mush. Bake, uncovered, 1 hour, or until hot and bubbly. Top with grated cheese and continue baking until cheese is melted and lightly browned.

🎵 **Good Idea: This pie freezes beautifully and thus can be made in advance. Cool the meat mixture before spooning it over the cornmeal. Finish assembling pie. Wrap in moistureproof or vaporproof wrap. Seal, label, and freeze. To serve, unwrap casserole. Cover and bake in a preheated 375° F. oven 1 hour and 30 minutes. Top with grated cheese and continue baking, uncovered, 15 minutes longer, or until piping hot.**

## GREEK NUT CAKE

20 to 24 squares

8 slices zwieback
1 (11½-ounce) can SOLO Nut Filling
1 (11½-ounce) can SOLO Pecan Filling
½ cup finely chopped walnuts
Finely grated peel of 1 orange
6 eggs, separated
½ teaspoon vanilla extract

Preheat oven to 350° F. Butter a 9½- x 13- x 2-inch baking pan. Put zwieback through an electric blender to make fine crumbs. Set aside. Combine nut filling, pecan filling, walnuts, and orange peel. Beat egg whites until they stand in stiff peaks. Beat egg yolks until well blended. Add nut fillings mixture to egg yolks and beat until mixture is smooth and well blended. Beat in vanilla. Fold in zwieback crumbs. Carefully fold in egg whites, retaining as much incorporated air as possible. Carefully spoon mixture into prepared baking pan. Smooth out top with a rubber spatula. Bake 45 minutes. Remove from oven and let stand until cool before cutting.

## LAMB KABOBS

4 to 6 servings

2 tablespoons butter or margarine
2 large onions, finely chopped
½ clove garlic, minced
1 (12-ounce) can SOLO Apricot Filling
¼ cup water
1 teaspoon salt
¼ cup lemon juice
2 pounds lean lamb, cut into 1-inch cubes
2 green peppers, cut into 1-inch chunks
2 firm tomatoes, cut into wedges
Hot cooked rice

In a saucepan, melt butter or margarine. Add onions and garlic and cook until soft but not browned. Add apricot filling, water, salt, and lemon juice. Stir to blend well. In a bowl, combine sauce and lamb cubes. Refrigerate several hours or overnight, stirring occasionally. To cook, remove meat from sauce and thread on skewers (at least 6 inches long), alternating with green pepper and tomato wedges. Preheat broiler. Place skewers on broiler pan and broil about 10 minutes, or to desired degree of doneness, turning occasionally. Brush with sauce during cooking time. Serve with hot cooked rice.

🍃Good Idea: For a festive meal, thread fresh apricot halves on the skewers alternately with the lamb cubes, green pepper, and tomatoes.

*Opposite: Lamb Kabobs and Baklava (page 40)*

## BAKLAVA 16 to 20 servings

*This is an old-favorite dessert, familiar to anyone who has ever eaten in a Greek, Armenian, or Turkish restaurant.*

| | |
|---|---|
| ½ **pound filo dough** | ½ **cup butter, clarified** * |
| 1 **(11½-ounce) can SOLO Nut Filling** | ¼ **cup margarine, clarified** * |
| ½ **cup finely chopped walnuts** | 1 **cup sugar** |
| ½ **teaspoon cinnamon** | 1 **cup water** |
| ¼ **teaspoon nutmeg** | 3 **slices lemon** |
| | 3 **tablespoons honey** |

Be sure filo dough has defrosted well in advance of using. (Let frozen or chilled dough stand at room temperature about 15 minutes.) Preheat oven to 350° F. Combine nut filling, walnuts, cinnamon, and nutmeg. Set aside. Brush the bottom of an 8-inch-square baking dish with part of the clarified butter and margarine. Cut filo dough into 8-inch-square sections. Brush dough with butter-margarine mixture. Layer ⅓ of the dough in bottom of pan. Top with one-half of the nut mixture. Cover with another ⅓ of the dough. Top with remaining nut mixture. Arrange remaining buttered layers of filo dough over top of nut filling. Using a sharp knife, cut, almost all the way through, into diamond shapes. Pour remaining butter-margarine mixture over top. Bake 1 hour. About 10 minutes before baklava is baked, combine sugar, 1 cup water, and lemon slices in a small saucepan. Bring to a boil and simmer about 5 minutes. Remove from heat, remove lemon slices, and stir in honey. Remove baklava from oven to pour hot honey syrup over top. Let stand at room temperature at least 2 hours—preferably more—before serving.

40

*To clarify butter and margarine, combine them in a small saucepan. Melt over low heat. Using a teaspoon, skim the bubbles from the top of the mixture and discard. Carefully pour the melted butter into a small bowl, leaving the white sediment on the bottom of the pan. Discard sediment, using just the clear butter mixture in the bowl. Use a pastry brush to brush the butter mixture on the filo dough.

**Good Idea: Filo dough, which is extremely thin and used in the baking of Greek delicacies, can be purchased in any gourmet shop or Near Eastern food store.**

## SWEET-SOUR MEAT LOAF

8 servings

1 (8-ounce) can tomato sauce
1 (10-ounce) jar SOLO Sweet and
   Sour Sauce
1 egg, well beaten
1 medium onion, minced

¼ cup cracker crumbs
2 pounds lean ground beef
1½ teaspoons salt
½ teaspoon pepper

Preheat oven to 400° F. Combine tomato sauce and sweet and sour sauce in a small bowl; set aside. Combine egg, onion, cracker crumbs, ground beef, salt, and pepper. Add ½ cup of the sweet and sour mixture and blend thoroughly. Turn meat mixture out into a shallow baking pan and shape into a round or oval loaf. Poke several finger-size holes in the top of the loaf. Pour remaining sweet and sour mixture over top. Bake 45 minutes, basting with sauce in pan several times during baking time.

**Good Idea:** To use your cooking fuel as economically as possible, bake potatoes at the same time you bake your meat loaf. For a new and unusual taste, skim off the fat that rises to the top of the sauce and serve it on the baked potatoes, or mix the skimmed-off fat with sour cream.

## SAUERBRATEN MEATBALLS

4 to 6 servings

1 pound lean ground beef
1 egg
¾ cup fresh bread crumbs
¼ cup water
¼ cup minced onion
½ teaspoon salt
⅛ teaspoon pepper

2 tablespoons butter or margarine
1 cup water
1 cup beef broth or bouillon
½ cup gingersnap crumbs
1 (10-ounce) jar SOLO Raisin
   Sauce

Combine meat, egg, bread crumbs, ¼ cup water, onion, salt, and pepper. Shape into balls about 1 inch in diameter. Melt butter or margarine in a heavy skillet and brown meatballs on all sides. Remove meatballs from skillet and add remaining ingredients. Bring mixture to a boil, stirring to loosen brown particles from bottom of pan. Lower heat. Return meatballs to pan and cover tightly. Simmer 20 to 25 minutes, or until meatballs are thoroughly cooked. Serve with mashed potatoes or potato dumplings.

## CHINESE CHICKEN AND VEGETABLES

3 to 4 servings

1 whole chicken breast, skinned
  and boned
2 tablespoons cooking oil
1 tablespoon soy sauce
1 tablespoon sherry
2 teaspoons cornstarch
1 teaspoon sugar
½ teaspoon ground ginger
2 (5/16-ounce) packages SOLO
  Dried Mushrooms

2 tablespoons cooking oil
2 cups thinly sliced celery
1 cup chicken broth
1 (5-ounce) can water chestnuts,
  drained and thinly sliced
2 tablespoons cornstarch
2 tablespoons cold water
½ cup thinly sliced green onions
  Hot cooked rice

Cut chicken breast into very thin slices along the grain of the meat. Combine 2 tablespoons oil, 1 tablespoon soy sauce, sherry, 2 teaspoons cornstarch, sugar, and ginger in a bowl. Add chicken slices and toss lightly. Prepare mushrooms according to package directions, reserving water in which they are soaked. Heat 2 tablespoons oil in a heavy skillet. Add chicken and cook, stirring occasionally, until chicken slices are opaque. Add celery and mushrooms and cook 2 minutes, stirring constantly. Add chicken broth and water from mushrooms. Cover and cook over moderate heat about 5 minutes, stirring several times, until mixture is well blended. Add water chestnuts and continue to cook until heated through. Combine 2 tablespoons cornstarch and cold water to make a smooth paste. Add to skillet and cook until mixture is smooth, clear, and thickened. Stir in onions and cook 1 minute. Serve with hot cooked rice and soy sauce.

43

Good Idea: The stir-fry method of cooking is fast and yields very good results. The best Chinese cooks recommend that you assemble all your utensils and prepare as many ingredients as you can before starting to stir-fry.

*Opposite: Sweet and Pungent Pork (page 44) and
Chinese Chicken and Vegetables*

## SWEET AND PUNGENT PORK

4 servings

2 large green peppers, cut into
   1-inch chunks
1 egg
2 tablespoons all-purpose flour
½ teaspoon salt
⅛ teaspoon pepper
1 pound lean pork, cut into
   ½-inch cubes

⅓ cup cooking oil
1 clove garlic
⅓ cup chicken bouillon
4 slices canned pineapple
1 (10-ounce) jar SOLO Sweet and
   Sour Sauce
Hot cooked rice

Cook green pepper in boiling water 4 to 5 minutes. Drain immediately and cool. Beat together egg, flour, salt, and pepper. Combine with pork cubes to coat each piece with batter. Place oil and garlic in a skillet and heat. Using a fork, remove each piece of pork from batter and drop into hot fat. Brown carefully on all sides. Remove pork pieces with a slotted spoon and discard oil and garlic. Return pork to skillet and add chicken bouillon. Cover and simmer about 8 minutes, or until pork is tender. Cut each pineapple slice into 8 to 10 pieces. Add to cooked pork with green pepper and heat, stirring, until peppers and pineapple are heated. Add sweet and sour sauce and heat just until hot. Serve immediately with hot cooked rice.

## RUSSIAN PORK CHOPS

6 servings

6 loin pork chops, cut ¾-inch
   thick
¼ cup all-purpose flour
¾ teaspoon salt
⅛ teaspoon pepper
¼ cup fine dry bread crumbs
2 tablespoons butter or margarine
1 (12-ounce) can SOLO Cherry
   Filling

1 teaspoon grated lemon peel
1 tablespoon lemon juice
½ teaspoon ground cinnamon
⅛ teaspoon ground cloves
½ cup water
½ cup port wine

Trim as much fat as possible from pork chops. Put chops into boiling salted water and simmer 15 minutes. Drain thoroughly and pat dry with paper towels. Combine flour, salt, and pepper. Dust chops with flour. Pat dry bread crumbs on both sides of chops. Melt butter or margarine in a heavy skillet over moderate heat. Sauté chops on both sides until lightly browned. Cook gently for 15 minutes, turning chops once during cooking time. In a saucepan, combine remaining ingredients and simmer gently. If sauce becomes too thick, add more water. To serve, spoon sauce over pork chops.

**Good Idea: A delicious accompaniment to these pork chops is cold sauerkraut mixed with grated carrots and a little salad oil.**

## SAVORY RED CABBAGE                    6 to 8 servings

| | |
|---|---|
| 1 **large head red cabbage** (about 2 pounds) | 3 **tablespoons butter or margarine** |
| 2 **tablespoons vinegar** | ¼ **cup chopped onion** |
| ½ **teaspoon salt** | ½ **(12-ounce) can SOLO Pineapple Filling** |
| 1 **cup water** | 1 **tablespoon lemon juice** |

45

Coarsely shred cabbage, discarding core. In a saucepan, combine vinegar, salt, and water. Bring to a boil. Add cabbage. Heat to boiling. Reduce heat and cook, covered, 10 minutes, or until cabbage is crisply tender. Drain thoroughly. Melt butter or margarine in a saucepan. Add onion and cook until tender. Add pineapple filling and lemon juice. Add cabbage and cook over low heat just until ingredients are blended.

**Good Idea: You can also make a delicious red cabbage dish by substituting ½ cup Solo Sweet and Sour Sauce for the pineapple filling and lemon juice. Simply toss the shredded, cooked cabbage lightly in the sweet and sour sauce, then heat and serve.**

## DANISH PORK CHOPS

4 servings

4 pork chops, cut ¾ inch thick
1 tablespoon butter or margarine
2 large apples, cored, peeled, and chopped
½ (12-ounce) can SOLO Prune Filling

½ cup chicken bouillon
½ cup heavy cream
Salt and pepper

Trim as much fat as possible from pork chops. Melt butter or margarine in a heavy skillet. Add pork chops and brown lightly on both sides. Add apples, prune filling, bouillon, and cream. Season lightly with salt and pepper. Cover and simmer 45 minutes, or until chops are tender. Stir sauce occasionally and, if sauce becomes too thick, add a little water. Remove chops. Skim off as much fat as possible from top of gravy and press through a sieve. Heat thoroughly and serve with chops.

✐ Good Idea: Serve this very rich dish with mashed potatoes or noodles covered with the extra gravy.

## 46  DANISH DOUGHNUTS

about 2 dozen

*(Aebleskivers)*

2 cups buttermilk
2 eggs, separated
2 cups all-purpose flour
½ teaspoon salt
1 teaspoon sugar

1 teaspoon baking soda
Sugar
1 (12-ounce) can SOLO Prune or other fruit filling

Beat buttermilk and egg yolks together. Sift together flour, salt, 1 teaspoon sugar, and baking soda. Stir into buttermilk mixture. Beat egg whites until stiff but not dry. Fold into buttermilk batter. Heat the aebleskiver pan. Brush with butter or margarine, using enough to leave a small amount in bottom of each cup. Fill each hole in pan two-thirds full of batter and cook slowly, until bottom is lightly browned. Using a long skewer, turn the balls and lightly brown the uncooked side. Serve immediately with sugar and a dab of fruit filling.

✐ Good Idea: Aebleskiver pans are made of cast iron and have hemispherical depressions. They can be purchased in department stores, specialty shops, and in most Scandinavian stores. For a delicious variation on this recipe, drop a teaspoonful of Solo Prune or Poppy Filling into the batter of each doughnut before cooking.

*Opposite: Danish Pork Chops and Danish Doughnuts*

## RUSSIAN STUFFED CABBAGE

4 to 6 servings

1 large head cabbage
½ cup ground pork
1 cup cooked rice or pearl barley
1 medium onion, minced

Salt and pepper
½ cup beef bouillon
½ (10-ounce) jar SOLO Raisin
Sauce

Cut core from cabbage head. Place cabbage in boiling water and boil until leaves separate without tearing. Select 8 to 12 large leaves; trim off midribs so leaves will roll easily. Reserve remaining cabbage for later use. Combine pork, rice or barley, and onion; add salt and pepper to taste. Divide mixture among cabbage leaves. Roll leaves firmly around mixture, tucking edges inside to contain stuffing. Secure tightly with food picks or tie with thread. Arrange cabbage rolls close together in a skillet. Combine bouillon and raisin sauce, pour over rolls. Cover and simmer over low heat 45 to 50 minutes, or until cabbage is tender and pork is cooked. Check occasionally and, if necessary, add more bouillon to keep cabbage from sticking to skillet. Arrange cabbage rolls on a heated platter. Serve with sauce from skillet and plain boiled potatoes.

48

## CINNAMON NUT BALLS

about 4 dozen cookies

1 cup butter or margarine
1 teaspoon vanilla extract
1 teaspoon cinnamon
3 tablespoons sugar

1 (11½-ounce) can SOLO Nut
Filling
2 cups all-purpose flour

Cream butter or margarine, vanilla, cinnamon, and sugar together until light and fluffy. Stir in nut filling. Add flour and stir to make a stiff dough. Refrigerate dough for several hours, or until firm enough to handle. Preheat oven to 325° F. With lightly floured hands, shape dough into small balls, about 1 inch in diameter. Place on ungreased baking sheet. Bake 15 to 20 minutes, or just until very lightly browned. Remove carefully from baking sheet and cool on wire rack. Dust lightly with confectioners sugar while still warm, if desired.

**Good Idea: To dust with confectioners sugar, place a piece of waxed paper under rack on which cookies are cooling. Place a small amount of confectioners sugar in a small strainer and rub through with a spoon. The sugar that drops through onto the waxed paper can be returned to the strainer and used until all the sugar is gone.**

*Opposite: Russian Stuffed Cabbage and Cinnamon Nut Balls*

## HUNGARIAN NOODLES

4 servings

8 ounces fine egg noodles

¼ cup butter or margarine

2 tablespoons SOLO Whole Poppy
Seed, crushed

Cook noodles in boiling salted water according to package directions. Drain thoroughly. Toss with butter or margarine and poppy seed. Keep warm in top part of double boiler or serve immediately.

## POPPY ROLL
*(Strudel)*

2 coffee cake rolls

3 to 3½ cups all-purpose flour

1½ tablespoons sugar

½ teaspoon salt

1 package active dry yeast

½ cup dairy sour cream

¼ cup water

½ cup butter or margarine

2 eggs, at room temperature

1 (12-ounce) can SOLO Poppy
Filling

In large bowl of electric mixer, combine 1 cup flour, sugar, salt, and dry yeast. In a saucepan, combine sour cream, water, and butter or margarine. Heat over low heat until liquids are very warm (120 – 130° F.). (Butter or margarine need not melt entirely.) Gradually add to dry ingredients; beat mixture 2 minutes at medium speed of electric mixer, scraping bowl occasionally. Add eggs and ½ cup flour. Beat at high speed 2 minutes, scraping bowl occasionally. Stir in enough additional flour to make a soft dough. Turn out onto a lightly floured board; knead a few times to form a ball. Cover and let stand 10 minutes. Divide dough in half. Roll each half out into a 14- x 12-inch rectangle. Spread each with ½ can of filling. Roll each up from one side, jelly-roll fashion. Seal edges. Place on greased baking sheet, sealed edges down. Cover and let rise in a warm place, free from draft, until doubled in bulk, about 1 hour. Preheat oven to 350° F. Bake about 35 minutes, or until lightly browned. Remove from baking sheet and cool on wire rack. When cool, drizzle with confectioners sugar icing, if desired.

**Good Idea: For an unusual variation, try Solo Nut Roll. Substitute 1 (11½-ounce) can nut or 1 (11½-ounce) can pecan filling for the poppy filling and proceed as directed in recipe. While still warm, sprinkle top of rolls with confectioners sugar or drizzle with confectioners sugar topping and a few chopped nuts.**

*Opposite: Hungarian Noodles and Poppy Roll*

## STUFFED PORK ROAST

8 servings

- 1 8-chop pork loin roast, center cut (about 4 pounds)
- ½ cup chopped onion
- ½ cup chopped celery
- ½ (8-ounce) package herb-seasoned stuffing mix
- ¼ cup snipped parsley
- ½ teaspoon salt
- ⅛ teaspoon pepper
- 1 (12-ounce) can SOLO Apricot Filling
- 1 cup apple sauce, chilled

Preheat oven to 325° F. Cut excess fat from roast. Fry fat in a skillet until some has been rendered. Discard remaining pieces of fat. Add onion and celery to skillet and sauté until soft but not browned. Add stuffing mix, parsley, salt, pepper, and three-fourths of the can of apricot filling. If mixture seems dry, add about 2 tablespoons hot water. From the fat side of the roast, cut down through meat to bone to make 8 chops. Spoon stuffing mixture into slits in roast and pat down gently. Bake about 2½ hours, or until meat is browned and tender. Cover top of roast with aluminum foil during last 20 to 30 minutes of cooking time, so that stuffing will not get too brown. To serve, cut through bone to separate chops; top with stuffing. Combine remaining apricot filling with chilled apple sauce and serve with meat.

## FINNISH ALMOND APPLES

4 servings

- 4 medium baking apples, peeled and cored
- ½ cup SOLO Almond Filling
- ½ cup all-purpose flour
- 1 cup corn flake crumbs
- 2 eggs, lightly beaten
- ¼ cup butter or margarine
  Heavy cream

Preheat oven to 350° F. Stuff apples with almond filling. Place flour and corn flake crumbs on separate pieces of waxed paper. Dip apples in flour, then in beaten eggs, and finally roll in corn flake crumbs, pressing crumbs in to cover apple smoothly. Place in a baking dish, with apples almost touching. Melt butter or margarine and pour over apples. Bake 45 minutes to 1 hour, or until apples are tender. Baste frequently during last 30 minutes of baking, so that crusts will brown lightly. Serve warm or cool with heavy pouring cream.

Good Idea: For a different flavor, serve the apples topped with a custard sauce that is lightly flavored with almond extract.

## FISH BAKED IN SAFFRON CREAM

| | |
|---|---|
| 1 or 2 (.01-ounce) packages SOLO Saffron | ¼ cup butter or margarine |
| 1 tablespoon hot water | ½ cup milk |
| ½ teaspoon salt | ½ cup dairy sour cream |
| ⅛ teaspoon pepper | ¼ cup buttered fine dry bread crumbs |
| 3 tablespoons all-purpose flour | |
| 1 pound fresh or frozen fish fillets, thawed | |

Crush saffron with fingers. Add hot water and let stand 30 minutes. Combine salt and pepper with 2 tablespoons of the flour. Coat fish fillets on both sides. Heat 3 tablespoons of the butter or margarine in a heavy skillet. Fry fish about 3 minutes on each side, or until lightly browned. Remove from skillet and place in a baking dish. Preheat oven to 400° F. Melt remaining butter in skillet. Add remaining flour and cook 30 seconds. Remove from heat and stir in milk. Return to heat and cook, stirring constantly, until mixture comes to a boil and is thickened. Lower heat and add sour cream. Heat but do not boil. Strain saffron through a fine sieve; add the liquid to sauce. Pour over top of fish in baking dish. Sprinkle with bread crumbs. Bake 10 to 15 minutes, or until fish flakes easily when tested with a fork and top is lightly browned.

53

Good Idea: This is an adaptation of a Russian dish that calls for porgies, but any kind of fish fillet can be used. The sour cream taste is accented by the saffron, making the dish very pleasant and highly enjoyable. Serve with a salad of cooked green peas, diced fresh cucumber, and a light french dressing, and with boiled potatoes and dark rye bread and butter.

## SHRIMP CURRY

2 to 3 servings

1 tablespoon butter or margarine
½ cup chopped onion
2 teaspoons curry powder
½ teaspoon salt
1 tablespoon lemon juice

1 (10-ounce) jar SOLO Raisin
   Sauce
1 tart apple, cored and chopped
1 cup cooked shrimp
Hot cooked rice

Melt butter or margarine in a large skillet and sauté onion until transparent. Add curry powder and cook until onion is tender but not browned. Add salt, lemon juice, raisin sauce, and chopped apple. Simmer 5 minutes. Add shrimp and heat. Serve over hot cooked rice.

**Good Idea: For condiments, provide bowls of chutney, Solo Coconut Flake, salted nuts, and chopped hard-cooked eggs.**

## SWEET POTATO-SAUSAGE CASSEROLE

4 to 5 servings

54

3 cups mashed sweet potatoes or
   yams (about 2½ pounds)
1 egg, lightly beaten
½ teaspoon salt

1 (12-ounce) can SOLO Apricot
   Filling
1 (8-ounce) package precooked
   sausages

Preheat oven to 375° F. Combine mashed sweet potatoes, egg, salt, and apricot filling. Beat until fluffy. Spoon into a lightly greased 1-quart casserole. Top with precooked sausages. Bake 30 to 35 minutes, or until piping hot and heated through.

*Opposite: Shrimp Curry*

# The Cookie Jar

## POPPY SEED COOKIES

about 4 dozen

| | |
|---|---|
| 1 cup butter or margarine | ⅛ teaspoon salt |
| ½ cup sugar | 3 tablespoons SOLO Whole Poppy |
| 2 egg yolks | Seed |
| 1 teaspoon vanilla extract | 1 (12-ounce) can SOLO Raspberry |
| 2 cups all-purpose flour | or Apricot Filling |

Cream butter or margarine and sugar together until fluffy. Beat in egg yolks and vanilla and blend well. Stir in flour, salt, and poppy seed and mix well. Refrigerate dough several hours or overnight. Preheat oven to 375° F. With lightly floured fingers, shape dough into 1-inch balls and place on ungreased baking sheets. Press in the center of each cookie with thumb or back of measuring teaspoon. Bake 12 to 15 minutes. Remove from oven; press in hollow on cookies while still warm. Just before serving, fill centers with desired filling.

## CRUNCHY POPPY BALLS

2½ to 3 dozen

1 cup butter or margarine
½ cup brown sugar, firmly
   packed
½ cup granulated sugar
½ (12-ounce) can SOLO Poppy
   Filling

1 egg, lightly beaten
2 cups all-purpose flour
¼ teaspoon baking soda
½ teaspoon salt
¾ cup corn flake crumbs
½ cup chopped nuts

Preheat oven to 350° F. Lightly grease a baking sheet. Cream butter or margarine, brown sugar, and granulated sugar together until fluffy. Add poppy filling and egg and blend well. In a separate bowl, combine flour, baking soda, salt, and crumbs. Add to poppy mixture and blend thoroughly. Add nuts. Shape mixture into balls about 1 inch in diameter. Place on baking sheet. Bake 15 minutes, or until lightly browned. Remove to wire rack. Drizzle with confectioners sugar icing while still warm, if desired.

## POPPY SEED COCONUT BARS

16 bars

1 cup all-purpose flour
⅛ teaspoon salt
⅛ teaspoon baking soda
½ cup plus 2 tablespoons sugar
¼ cup butter or margarine,
   melted
3 tablespoons honey

½ teaspoon vanilla extract
2 egg whites
1 tablespoon milk
½ cup SOLO Coconut Flake
1 tablespoon SOLO Whole Poppy
   Seed

Preheat oven to 350° F. Butter a 9-inch-square baking pan. Line pan with waxed paper and butter again. Sift together flour, salt, baking soda, and sugar. Add butter or margarine, honey, vanilla, egg whites, and milk and stir thoroughly. Stir in coconut. Spread batter evenly in bottom of prepared pan. Sprinkle poppy seed over top of batter. Bake 25 to 30 minutes, or until top is firm when pressed lightly with fingers. Cool in pan about 5 minutes. Turn out of pan onto wire rack and peel off paper. When completely cooled, cut into 16 bars. Store in an airtight container.

## CHOW MEIN DATE SQUARES

about 30 squares

*This is an unusual cookie. The noodles on top give it a crunchy texture as well as a distinctive taste.*

1 cup brown sugar, firmly
    packed
1½ cups all-purpose flour
½ teaspoon salt
¾ cup butter or margarine

1 (12-ounce) can SOLO Date
    Filling
1 (3-ounce) can chow mein
    noodles

Preheat oven to 375° F. Combine brown sugar, flour, and salt. Add butter or margarine and mix with fingers, or blend in with two knives, until mixture is crumbly. Pat mixture in bottom of a lightly greased 13- x 9-inch baking pan. Cover with date filling. Sprinkle noodles over top of filling. Pat down lightly so that noodles adhere to dates. Bake 30 to 35 minutes, or until nicely browned. (This is a heavy dough, so be sure center of cookie dough is done before removing from oven.) Remove from oven and cool. When cool, cut into squares.

## 58 ALMOND CHINESE CHEWS

about 3 dozen

1 cup sugar
3 eggs, lightly beaten
1 (12-ounce) can SOLO Almond
    Filling

¾ cup all-purpose flour
1 teaspoon baking powder
¼ teaspoon salt
    Confectioners sugar

Preheat oven to 300° F. Grease a 13- x 9-inch baking pan. Add sugar to beaten eggs and continue beating until very well blended. Stir in almond filling. Sift together flour, baking powder, and salt. Lightly fold into egg mixture. Pour into prepared pan. Bake 40 to 45 minutes, or until a cake tester inserted in center comes out clean. Let stand in pan until cool. Cut into rectangles and dust lightly with confectioners sugar before serving.

**Good Idea: This is almost more of a cake than a cookie, with a moist, spongy texture. If you like an added crispness, add ½ cup finely chopped blanched almonds to the batter before pouring into pan.**

## ALMOND CRESCENTS

about 4 dozen

1 cup butter or margarine
⅓ cup sugar
1 teaspoon almond extract
1 (12-ounce) can SOLO Almond
   Filling

2 cups all-purpose flour
Confectioners sugar

Cream butter or margarine, sugar, and almond extract together until light and fluffy. Add filling and mix well. Add flour and stir well to make a stiff dough. Refrigerate dough 3 to 4 hours, or until it is firm enough to handle easily. Preheat oven to 325° F. With floured hands, shape small amounts of dough into small rolls, about 2½ inches in length. Place on ungreased baking sheets and form into crescents. Bake 15 to 20 minutes, or until set and lightly browned. Remove carefully from baking sheets and cool on wire rack. While still slightly warm, dust with confectioners sugar.*

*See Good Idea on page 48.

## ALMOND MACAROONS

3½ to 4 dozen

1 (8-ounce) can SOLO Almond
   Paste

2 egg whites
1¼ cups sugar

Preheat oven to 325° F. Cover a baking sheet with brown paper. Cut almond paste up into small pieces in a mixing bowl. Add egg whites and sugar and blend until mixture is very smooth. Using a pastry bag with star tube, pipe out cookies about the size of half dollars, or drop by spoonfuls, onto brown paper on baking sheet. Bake 25 to 30 minutes, or until lightly browned. Remove cookies carefully from paper when cool. If they do not come off easily, wet the back of the paper and they will loosen.

**Good Idea: If you like a chewy macaroon, bake 25 minutes. For a crisper macaroon, bake 30 minutes. Always store these macaroons in an airtight can.**

## DUTCH ALMOND ROLLETTES

*(Bonket)*

8 dozen

| | |
|---|---|
| 1 cup butter or margarine, softened | 1 egg, lightly beaten |
| 2 cups sifted all-purpose flour | ¾ cup sugar |
| ¼ cup ice water | 1 (8-ounce) can SOLO Almond Paste |

Using a pastry blender or two knives, cut butter or margarine into flour. Add ice water gradually, mixing well. Refrigerate to chill thoroughly. Combine egg, sugar, and almond paste; refrigerate to chill. Preheat oven to 400° F. Divide dough into four portions. On a lightly floured board, roll each portion into a 12- x 4-inch rectangle. On a lightly floured cloth, turn out almond mixture and shape into four rolls about 11 inches long. Place one roll of almond mixture on each pastry rectangle. Brush one long edge with water; roll pastry around filling, rolling toward the wet edge. Place rolls, seam side down, on ungreased baking sheets. Prick with a fork, and brush with diluted egg yolk, if desired. Bake 15 minutes. Reduce oven temperature to 325° F. and bake 20 minutes longer. When rolls are cool, cut into ½-inch slices.

60 **Good Idea: You can make these cookies with 1 (12-ounce) can Almond Filling by omitting the egg and sugar and proceeding as directed.**

## COCONUT KISSES

about 4 dozen

| | |
|---|---|
| ½ teaspoon salt | 1 teaspoon vanilla extract |
| 4 egg whites | 2 cups SOLO Coconut Flake |
| 1¼ cups sugar | |

Preheat oven to 350° F. Add salt to egg whites and beat until stiff but not dry. Add sugar, 1 tablespoon at a time, beating until all sugar is dissolved. Add vanilla and coconut, mixing lightly. Cover ungreased baking sheet with brown paper. Drop mixture by teaspoonfuls onto paper. Bake about 20 minutes. Slip paper off of baking sheet and onto wet table or board. Let stand 1 minute. Loosen cookies with spatula; remove to wire rack. Top each with a candied cherry half, if desired.

**Good Idea: It isn't necessary to buy a roll of brown paper just to make these cookies. Use brown paper bags from the grocery store; when the bags are cut open they are just the right size.**

## APRICOT COCONUT BALLS

about 36 balls

¼ cup butter or margarine
6 tablespoons sugar
½ (12-ounce) can SOLO Apricot
Filling
1 egg yolk

2 cups crisp rice cereal
½ teaspoon vanilla extract
½ cup finely chopped nuts
2½ cups SOLO Coconut Flake

Melt butter or margarine in a heavy saucepan over low heat. Add sugar, apricot filling, and egg yolk and blend well. Cook over very low heat, stirring, until mixture just comes to a boil. Remove from heat and stir in cereal, vanilla, and nuts. Drop by teaspoonfuls into coconut flake and roll to coat. Store in refrigerator.


## BOHEMIAN FRUIT SLICES

about 3 dozen

*This is a cross between a cookie and a coffee cake. No matter what you call it, it's great with coffee in the morning or with coffee or tea in the afternoon.*

¼ cup warm water (105 – 115° F.)
1 package active dry yeast
2 cups all-purpose flour
¼ cup sugar
½ teaspoon salt

¾ cup butter or margarine
1 egg
1 (12-ounce) can SOLO Prune
Filling
Confectioners sugar

Preheat oven to 375° F. Measure water in a small warm cup or bowl. Add yeast and stir until yeast is dissolved. Let stand. Combine flour, sugar, and salt in a mixing bowl. With a pastry blender or two knives, cut in butter or margarine until mixture resembles coarse cornmeal. Add egg and yeast and blend until dough sticks together. Shape into a smooth ball with the fingers. Divide dough in half. Roll out each half on a lightly floured board into a 13- x 9-inch rectangle. Spread each half with half a can of prune filling. Roll up, jelly-roll fashion, from the long side. Pinch edges together and place on a lightly greased baking sheet, seam sides down. With a sharp knife, make a ½-inch-deep cut lengthwise down the center of each roll. Bake 25 to 30 minutes, or until lightly browned. Remove from oven and sprinkle with confectioners sugar while still warm. Cut into diagonal slices, about ¾ inch thick, before serving.

## APRICOT SLICES

about 2 dozen

1 cup butter or margarine, softened
2 cups sifted all-purpose flour
1 cup dairy sour cream

1 (12-ounce) can SOLO Apricot Filling
1 cup SOLO Coconut Flake
1 cup chopped pecans
Confectioners sugar

Using a pastry blender or two knives, cut butter or margarine into flour. Add sour cream and blend. Refrigerate to chill thoroughly. Preheat oven to 350° F. Divide dough into four portions. On a lightly floured board, roll each portion into a 12- x 6-inch rectangle. Spread each with apricot filling and sprinkle with coconut and pecans. Roll each rectangle up from 6-inch end, jelly-roll fashion. Place on ungreased baking sheet. Bake about 45 minutes. While still warm, sprinkle each roll liberally with confectioners sugar. When cool, cut into 1-inch slices.

## EUROPEAN PRUNE KOLACKY

about 3 dozen

*The kolacky are traditional European tarts or cookies that have become popular in America. Make them with any Solo filling or glaze—they're equally delicious!*

1 cup butter or margarine, softened
1 (8-ounce) package cream cheese, softened
1 tablespoon milk
1 tablespoon sugar

1 egg yolk, well beaten
1½ cups all-purpose flour
½ teaspoon baking powder
1 (12-ounce) can SOLO Prune Filling
Confectioners sugar

Cream butter or margarine, cream cheese, milk, and sugar together. Add egg yolk. Sift together flour and baking powder. Add to creamed mixture and blend well. Refrigerate for several hours or overnight. Preheat oven to 400° F. Turn dough out on a lightly floured board and roll to a ¼-inch thickness. Cut with a cookie sheet and make a depression with thumb or spoon in center of each. Place 1 teaspoon prune filling into each center. Bake 10 to 12 minutes, or until lightly browned. Sprinkle with confectioners sugar before serving.

*Opposite: European Prune Kolacky (made with Cherry Filling), Date-Filled Cookie Log (page 64), and Coconut Macaroons (page 64)*

## DATE-FILLED COOKIE LOG

about 4 dozen

½ cup butter or margarine
1 cup brown sugar, firmly
  packed
1 egg, well beaten
2 cups all-purpose flour
¼ teaspoon salt

¼ teaspoon baking soda
1 (12-ounce) can SOLO Date
  Filling
½ cup finely chopped nuts
Confectioners sugar

Preheat oven to 400° F. Cream butter or margarine and sugar together. Stir in egg and blend well. Sift together flour, salt, and baking soda. Add to creamed mixture and blend to make a stiff dough. Divide dough into four parts. Shape into logs, about 10 inches long and 3 inches wide, on baking sheet. Make an indentation down center of each log with the side of the hand. Spread ¼ cup date filling in each indentation. Sprinkle with nuts. Bake 12 to 15 minutes, or until logs are set and lightly browned. Remove from oven and let cool. While still slightly warm, cut at an angle into ¾-inch slices. Sprinkle with confectioners sugar.

64

**Good Idea: Be sure to place no more than two logs on a baking sheet, because they will spread slightly while baking.**

## COCONUT MACAROONS

2½ dozen

2 egg whites
½ teaspoon salt
1 cup sugar

½ cup SOLO Coconut Flake
1½ cups corn flakes
1 teaspoon vanilla extract

Preheat oven to 325° F. Beat egg whites and salt together just until stiff. Gradually beat in sugar, a small amount at a time, beating until sugar is dissolved and whites stand in stiff peaks. Fold in coconut, corn flakes, and vanilla. Drop by teaspoonfuls onto greased baking sheet. Bake about 20 minutes, or until golden brown and set. Remove from sheet and cool on wire rack.

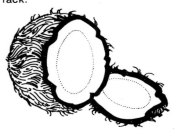

## RAISIN SAUCE OATMEAL COOKIES

about 5 dozen

| | |
|---|---|
| ¾ cup butter or margarine | 1 teaspoon salt |
| 1¼ cups sugar | 1 teaspoon baking soda |
| 1 egg | 1 teaspoon cinnamon |
| 1 (10-ounce) jar SOLO Raisin Sauce | 2 cups quick-cooking rolled oats |
| 1¾ cups all-purpose flour | ½ cup chopped walnuts |

Preheat oven to 375° F. Cream butter or margarine and sugar together until fluffy. Add egg and beat well. Stir in raisin sauce. Sift together flour, salt, baking soda, and cinnamon. Add to creamed mixture. Stir in oats and walnuts. Drop by teaspoonfuls, about 2 inches apart, onto lightly greased baking sheet. Bake 10 to 15 minutes, or until lightly browned. Remove from oven and let stand on baking sheet about 1 minute. Remove from sheet and cool on wire rack.

## PINEAPPLE OATMEAL COOKIES

6 dozen

| | |
|---|---|
| ¾ cup butter or margarine | ½ teaspoon baking soda |
| 1 cup sugar | ½ teaspoon salt |
| 2 eggs | 1 (12-ounce) can SOLO Pineapple Filling |
| 1 teaspoon grated lemon peel | |
| 2 cups all-purpose flour | 2 cups quick-cooking rolled oats |
| 1 teaspoon baking powder | |

Preheat oven to 375° F. Cream butter or margarine and sugar together until fluffy. Add eggs and lemon peel and beat well. Sift together flour, baking powder, baking soda, and salt. Add to creamed mixture alternately with pineapple filling. Stir in oats and blend well. Drop by teaspoonfuls, about 2 inches apart, on a lightly greased baking sheet. Bake 15 to 16 minutes, or until lightly browned on the bottom and set. Let stand 1 minute, then remove from baking sheet and cool on wire rack.

**Good Idea: For a tempting nutty taste, add ⅓ cup Solo Nut Filling along with the oats.**

## OATMEAL DATE COOKIES

about 7 dozen

1 cup butter or margarine
1 cup sugar
1 teaspoon vanilla extract
2 cups quick-cooking rolled
   oats
2 cups all-purpose flour

¼ teaspoon baking soda
¾ teaspoon salt
½ cup buttermilk
1 (12-ounce) can SOLO Date
   Filling

Cream butter or margarine and sugar together until fluffy. Stir in vanilla and rolled oats. Sift together flour, baking soda, and salt. Add to oatmeal mixture alternately with buttermilk and blend well. Refrigerate dough several hours or overnight. Preheat oven to 400° F. On a lightly floured board, roll chilled dough, a small amount at a time, out to about a ⅛-inch thickness. Cut into rounds with a 1½- to 2-inch cookie cutter. Place on a lightly greased baking sheet and bake 8 to 10 minutes, or until lightly browned and set. Put cookies together with date filling, sandwich fashion, when ready to serve.

## SOUR CREAM DATE DROPS

about 6 dozen

¼ cup butter or margarine
¾ cup brown sugar, firmly
   packed
½ teaspoon vanilla extract
1 egg
1 (12-ounce) can SOLO Date
   Filling
1½ cups all-purpose flour

½ teaspoon baking soda
¼ teaspoon baking powder
¼ teaspoon salt
¼ teaspoon cinnamon
⅛ teaspoon nutmeg
½ cup dairy sour cream
   Walnut halves or quarters

Preheat oven to 375° F. Cream butter or margarine and sugar together until fluffy. Add vanilla and egg and mix well. Stir in date filling. Sift together flour, baking soda, baking powder, salt, cinnamon, and nutmeg. Add to creamed mixture alternately with sour cream. Blend well. Drop by teaspoonfuls onto a lightly greased baking sheet. Press a walnut half or quarter on top of each cookie. Bake 12 to 15 minutes, or until lightly browned on the bottom and set. Let stand on baking sheet about 1 minute, then remove and cool on wire rack.

Good Idea: This cookie is moist and chewy and keeps well. Any kind of nuts can be used or they can be omitted altogether, though they add a special flavor and bite to the cookie.

## DATE SWIRLS

5 to 6 dozen

⅓ cup butter or margarine
½ cup brown sugar, firmly
    packed
½ cup granulated sugar
½ teaspoon vanilla extract
1 egg

2 cups all-purpose flour
¼ teaspoon baking soda
⅛ teaspoon salt
1 (12-ounce) can SOLO Date
    Filling
½ cup finely chopped nuts

Cream butter or margarine and sugars together until fluffy. Add vanilla and egg and beat well. Sift together flour, baking soda, and salt. Add to creamed mixture and blend well. Refrigerate dough until firm enough to handle. Divide dough in half. On lightly floured waxed paper, roll out each half into a 9- x 12-inch rectangle. Combine date filling and nuts. Spread half of the mixture on each half of the dough. Roll dough up tightly, jelly-roll fashion, from long end. Wrap tightly in waxed paper. Refrigerate overnight. Preheat oven to 375° F. Cut rolls into ⅛-inch-thick slices and place on lightly greased baking sheet. Bake 10 minutes. Remove from baking sheet and cool on wire rack.

## DATE DIAMONDS

18 to 20 cookies

1 (12-ounce) can SOLO Date
    Filling
½ cup chopped walnuts
1¾ cups quick-cooking rolled
    oats

½ cup brown sugar, firmly
    packed
¾ cup all-purpose flour
¼ teaspoon salt
¾ cup butter or margarine

Preheat oven to 350°F. Lightly butter an 8- or 9-inch-square pan. Combine date filling and walnuts and mix well. Set aside. Combine rolled oats, brown sugar, flour, and salt and blend well. Cut in butter or margarine with two knives, or mix in with fingers, until mixture is crumbly. Pat two-thirds of the mixture in bottom of prepared pan. Spread date filling over top of mixture. Sprinkle remaining oat mixture over date mixture and pat lightly into filling. Bake 35 to 40 minutes, or until lightly browned. Let stand in pan until cool, then cut into diamond shapes.

**Good Idea: For ease in spreading thick filling over a crumbly dough, drop filling by spoonfuls onto top of dough and use a spatula lightly to smooth it out, dipping the spatula into warm water occasionally so that it does not pull the filling from the dough.**

## SOLO PECAN SQUARES

3 dozen

½ cup butter or margarine
3 tablespoons granulated sugar
1 cup all-purpose flour
2 eggs
1 (11½-ounce) can SOLO Pecan Filling
1 cup brown sugar, firmly packed

½ teaspoon vanilla extract
2½ tablespoons all-purpose flour
1½ teaspoons baking powder
¼ teaspoon salt
½ cup quick-cooking rolled oats
½ cup SOLO Coconut Flake

Preheat oven to 375° F. Cream butter or margarine and granulated sugar together until fluffy. Add flour and mix to make a crumbly dough. Turn into a lightly greased 9-inch-square baking pan. Pat out with fingers to cover bottom of pan. Bake 15 minutes. Remove from oven and reduce heat to 350° F. Beat eggs lightly. Beat in pecan filling and brown sugar and blend until smooth. Stir in vanilla. Sift together flour, baking powder, and salt. Stir into egg mixture. Fold in rolled oats and coconut flake. Spread over top of baked cookie layer. Bake 35 to 45 minutes longer, or until a cake tester inserted in center comes out clean. Cool thoroughly before cutting into squares.

## PECAN BROWNIES

about 4 dozen

½ cup butter or margarine
1 cup sugar
1 (11½-ounce) can SOLO Pecan Filling
2 eggs

1¼ cups all-purpose flour
⅛ teaspoon salt
½ teaspoon baking powder
½ teaspoon baking soda

Preheat oven to 350° F. Grease and lightly flour a 13- x 9-inch baking pan. Cream butter or margarine and sugar together until light and fluffy. Add pecan filling and blend well. Add eggs and beat well. Sift together flour, salt, baking powder, and baking soda. Stir into creamed mixture and blend well. Turn into prepared pan. Bake 35 to 40 minutes, until lightly browned, or until a cake tester inserted in center comes out clean. Remove from oven and let cool before cutting into squares. Brownies may be frosted or lightly dusted with confectioners sugar, if desired.

**Good Idea: To make chocolate pecan brownies, sift 2 tablespoons cocoa in with the dry ingredients.**

## THUMBPRINT COOKIES

about 2 dozen

½ cup butter or margarine
¼ cup brown sugar, firmly packed
½ teaspoon vanilla extract
1 egg, separated
1 cup all-purpose flour

¼ teaspoon salt
¾ cup finely chopped nuts
1 (12-ounce) can SOLO Date or
   Apricot Filling

Preheat oven to 375° F. Cream butter or margarine, brown sugar, and vanilla together. Stir in egg yolk and mix well. Stir in flour and salt. With lightly floured fingers, roll dough into balls about 1 inch in diameter. Beat egg white slightly. Dip cookie dough balls into egg white and roll in nuts. Place on ungreased baking sheet. Press thumb into center of each cookie. Fill depression in cookie with desired filling. Bake 12 to 15 minutes, or until lightly browned and set. Remove from baking sheet and cool on wire rack. Add more filling, if desired, before serving cookies.

♫ **Good Idea: These cookies can be baked without filling and filled when they are cool. If you choose to follow this method, press depressions in cookies again when they are removed from the oven to allow enough room for the filling.**

## FILLED COOKIES

about 2½ dozen

½ cup butter or margarine
¾ cup sugar
1 egg
½ teaspoon vanilla extract
2¼ cups all-purpose flour
¼ teaspoon baking powder

½ teaspoon baking soda
½ teaspoon salt
½ cup dairy sour cream
1 (12-ounce) can SOLO Date or
   Prune Filling

Cream butter or margarine and sugar together until fluffy. Add egg and vanilla and blend well. Sift together flour, baking powder, baking soda, and salt. Add to creamed mixture alternately with sour cream. Blend well. Refrigerate dough until firm enough to handle. Preheat oven to 375° F. On a well-floured board and using a well-floured rolling pin, roll dough, a small amount at a time, to about a ¼-inch thickness. Cut into rounds with a 2½-inch cookie cutter. Place half of cookies on ungreased baking sheet. Place a teaspoonful of desired filling in center of each cookie. Top with another cookie and press edges together with a fork. Bake 12 to 15 minutes, or until lightly browned and set. Remove from baking sheet and cool on wire rack.

## LEMON BARS

16 to 20 bars

½ cup butter or margarine
1 cup all-purpose flour
¼ cup confectioners sugar

1⅓ cups SOLO Coconut Flake
1 (12-ounce) can SOLO Lemon
   Filling

Preheat oven to 350° F. Combine butter or margarine, flour, sugar, and ⅓ cup of the coconut flake. Rub mixture together with fingers until crumbly. Pat into bottom of a lightly greased 8- or 9-inch-square baking pan. Bake 10 minutes. Remove from oven and cool 5 minutes. Spread lemon filling over cookie crust. Sprinkle with remaining 1 cup coconut flake. Reduce oven temperature to 325° F. Bake 25 minutes longer. Cool before cutting into bars.

## RASPBERRY MERINGUES

about 4 dozen

1 cup butter or margarine
½ cup light brown sugar, firmly
   packed
1 egg
2 cups all-purpose flour
1 (12-ounce) can SOLO Raspberry
   Filling

3 egg whites
¾ cup sugar
½ cup SOLO Coconut Flake
½ cup slivered almonds

70

Preheat oven to 325° F. Cream butter or margarine and brown sugar together until fluffy. Add egg and blend well. Stir in flour to make a smooth dough. Pat dough into a lightly greased 13- x 9- x 2-inch pan. Bake 20 minutes. Remove from oven and spread with raspberry filling. Beat egg whites until frothy. Gradually beat in sugar and beat until stiff and glossy. Fold in coconut flake and almonds. Spread over raspberry filling. Return to oven and bake 20 minutes longer, or until meringue is lightly browned. Cool in pan. Cut into 1½-inch squares.

**Good Idea: For a delicious nutty taste, cream ½ cup Solo Almond Paste together with the butter or margarine and brown sugar.**

*Opposite: Lemon Bars and Raspberry Meringues*

## RASPBERRY WREATHS

about 2 dozen

1 cup butter or margarine
½ cup confectioners sugar
2 tablespoons milk
½ teaspoon vanilla extract

2¼ cups all-purpose flour
½ teaspoon salt
¼ teaspoon baking powder
½ cup SOLO Raspberry Filling

Cream butter or margarine and sugar together until fluffy. Stir in milk and vanilla. Sift together flour, salt, and baking powder. Add to creamed mixture and stir until well blended. Refrigerate dough several hours. Preheat oven to 350° F. On a lightly floured board, roll dough, a small amount at a time, to a ⅛-inch thickness. Cut with a 2-inch cookie cutter into 4 dozen rounds. Cut a 1-inch circle from half of the rounds to form 2 dozen rings. Place cookies and rings on lightly greased baking sheets. Bake 10 minutes, or until golden brown. Cool. Before serving, spread about 1 teaspoon filling on each of the cookie rounds. Top with the cookie rings.

## TEA TREATS

2 dozen

1 (3-ounce) package cream cheese,
    softened
½ cup butter or margarine
1 cup all-purpose flour
⅔ cup brown sugar, firmly
    packed

2 tablespoons all-purpose flour
⅛ teaspoon salt
1 egg, well beaten
1 teaspoon vanilla extract
½ (11½-ounce) can SOLO Nut
    Filling

Preheat oven to 350° F. Combine cream cheese and butter or margarine and blend well. Stir in 1 cup flour and blend to make a stiff dough. Form dough into 1-inch balls and place in 1¾-inch muffin pan cups, 1 ball to a cup. Press dough firmly against bottom and sides of cups. Combine sugar, 2 tablespoons flour, and salt. Add egg, vanilla, and nut filling and blend well. Divide mixture between prepared muffin cups. Bake 30 to 35 minutes, or until filling is set and crusts are lightly browned. Remove from oven and cool in cups.

**Good Idea: For a delicious variation, combine ¼ cup butter or margarine, melted, with 6 tablespoons sugar, 1 lightly beaten egg yolk, and ½ (12-ounce) can Solo Apricot Filling. Blend well. Use instead of nut filling to fill pastry cups. Bake until filling is set.**

## COTTAGE CHEESE POCKETS

3 dozen

1 cup butter or margarine
1 cup creamy cottage cheese
2 cups all-purpose flour

1 (12-ounce) can SOLO filling,
   any desired flavor
Confectioners sugar

Cream butter or margarine and cottage cheese together. Add flour and blend to make a smooth dough. Wrap dough in waxed paper and refrigerate several hours, or until dough is firm. When cold, divide dough in quarters. On a lightly floured board, roll one quarter at a time out into a 9-inch square. Cut each into nine 3-inch squares. Place a teaspoonful of desired filling in center of each square. Fold each corner to center and pinch corners together to seal, or fold two corners to center and pinch together, leaving other two ends open. Preheat oven to 425° F. Place cookies on baking sheet. Bake 12 to 15 minutes, or until puffed and lightly browned. Remove from oven and sprinkle with confectioners sugar while still warm.

## LORETTA'S DREAM BARS

about 4 dozen

1 cup butter or margarine
1 cup brown sugar, firmly
   packed
1 teaspoon vanilla extract
1 egg
2 cups all-purpose flour

½ teaspoon salt
1 teaspoon cinnamon
1 (12-ounce) can SOLO filling,
   any desired fruit flavor
Confectioners sugar

Preheat oven to 350° F. Grease and lightly flour the bottom of a 15- x 10-inch jelly roll pan. Cream butter or margarine and brown sugar together until fluffy. Stir in vanilla and egg and beat well. Sift together flour, salt, and cinnamon. Stir into creamed mixture and blend well. Spread mixture in prepared pan. Bake 25 to 30 minutes, or until lightly browned and set. Cool in pan. Spread with desired fruit filling. Cut into bars and sprinkle with confectioners sugar before serving.

# Pies & Pastries

2 crusts

| | |
|---|---|
| **2 cups all-purpose flour** | **⅔ cup shortening** |
| **1 teaspoon salt** | **¼ cup ice water** |

Sift together flour and salt. With a pastry blender or two knives, cut half the shortening into flour mixture until mixture has consistency of cornmeal. Cut in remaining shortening until particles are the size of small peas. Sprinkle ice water over top, 1 tablespoonful at a time. Toss lightly with a fork to make mixture hold together. Turn dough out onto a piece of waxed paper; press gently with hands to form a ball. Refrigerate until chilled.

*For a single crust:* Divide ball of dough in half. On a lightly floured board, roll dough into a circle about ⅛ inch thick. Roll lightly from the center out at all times. Fold dough in half, lift gently, and place in pie pan. Carefully unfold dough to fit into pan. Fit pastry by lifting and patting gently. Do not stretch the dough to make it fit or it will shrink down into pan when it is baked. Fold edges of crust under to make ridge. Flute edges by pressing index finger of one hand between thumb and index finger of other hand. For a baked shell, prick pastry all over with a fork to allow steam to escape. Bake in a very hot oven (450° F.) 12 to 15 minutes, or until crust is lightly browned. Check occasionally to see that crust is not sliding down into pan. If it is, press it gently back in place with the fingers. (To help prevent the crust from sliding, place a sheet of aluminum foil over the crust, fill with dry peas or beans, and bake about 10 minutes. Remove the foil and dry peas and continue baking until crust is lightly browned.)

**Sesame Pie Shell**

Add 1 tablespoon toasted sesame seed to flour and continue as above.

### EASY PIE CRUST                                         1 crust

| | |
|---|---|
| 1 cup plus 2 tablespoons all-purpose flour | ⅓ cup corn oil |
| | 2 tablespoons cold water |
| ½ teaspoon salt | |

Preheat oven to 450° F. Combine flour and salt. Blend in oil and mix thoroughly. Sprinkle water over mixture and blend well. Press dough firmly into a ball with the hands. (The dough will look and feel very oily.) If dough is too dry, add a little more oil. Flatten ball slightly and roll between 2 pieces of waxed paper into a circle about 12 inches in diameter. To keep paper from slipping during rolling, wipe table with damp cloth or sponge. Peel off top paper and replace lightly; flip pastry and papers over and peel off other paper. Place pastry in pie pan, paper side up. Peel off paper and fit pastry loosely into pan. Trim edges if necessary. Fold pastry under around edges, and flute edges with finger tips. Prick all over with a fork. Bake 12 to 15 minutes, or until lightly browned. If pastry is to be baked with a filling, do not prick before baking.

### GRAHAM CRACKER CRUST                                  1 crust

| | |
|---|---|
| 20 graham crackers (1½ cups crumbs) | ¼ cup softened butter or margarine |
| ¼ cup sugar | |

Preheat oven to 375° F. Place crackers in a plastic bag. With a rolling pin, roll out into fine crumbs. Pour crumbs into a bowl. Add sugar and butter or margarine and blend thoroughly. Pour crumb mixture into a 9-inch pie plate. Set an 8-inch pie plate on top of crumbs and press them firmly into an even layer against bottom and sides of pan. Bake 8 minutes. Cool well before filling with desired filling.

**Good Idea: For a tasty variation, add 1 tablespoon Solo Whole Poppy Seed to the crumb mixture.**

## PECAN PIE

1 (11½-ounce) can SOLO Pecan
   Filling
1 tablespoon sugar
2 tablespoons all-purpose flour

2 cups white corn syrup
4 eggs
1 unbaked 9-inch pie shell

Preheat oven to 425° F. Combine all ingredients, except pie shell. Mix until smooth and well blended. Pour into pie shell. Bake 15 minutes. Reduce heat to 350° F. and continue baking 30 minutes, or until a silver knife inserted in center of pie comes out clean. Cool. Serve with a dab of whipped cream and a few chopped pecans, if desired.

## FRUIT CHIFFON PIE

76

1 tablespoon (1 envelope)
   unflavored gelatine
¼ cup cold water
3 eggs, separated
½ cup sugar
¼ teaspoon salt
¼ cup orange juice

2 tablespoons lemon juice
1 tablespoon grated orange peel
   (optional)
1 (12-ounce) can SOLO Apricot
   or Prune Filling
6 tablespoons sugar
1 baked 9-inch pie shell

Soften gelatine in cold water. Beat egg yolks in a saucepan. Add ½ cup sugar, salt, orange juice, and lemon juice and beat well. Cook over low heat, stirring constantly, until mixture is thick and smooth. Remove from heat; add gelatine and stir until gelatine is dissolved. When mixture is cool, stir in orange peel and filling. Beat egg whites until stiff. Beat in 6 tablespoons sugar, 1 tablespoonful at a time, beating well after each addition. Fold egg whites into cooled fruit mixture. Blend lightly. Turn into baked pie shell. Refrigerate to chill thoroughly before serving.

♫ **Good Idea: Any Solo fruit filling can be used in this pie.**

## SOLO FRUIT-'N'-CREAM PIE

1 pie

1 (3¾-ounce) package vanilla
    pudding and pie filling mix
2 cups milk
1 baked 8- or 9-inch pie shell

1 (12-ounce) can SOLO Pineapple,
    Cherry, or Prune Filling
1 cup heavy cream, whipped

Prepare mix according to package directions for pie filling, using the 2 cups of milk. Cool thoroughly. Pour into baked pie shell. Spread desired filling over top. Serve with sweetened and flavored whipped cream.

## NO-BAKE CHERRY CHEESE PIE

1 9-inch pie

1 (8-ounce) package cream
    cheese, softened
1 (15-ounce) can sweetened
    condensed milk
⅓ cup lemon juice

1 (12-ounce) can SOLO Cherry
    Filling
1 baked 9-inch graham cracker
    crust (see page 75)

Beat cream cheese until soft and smooth. Add condensed milk slowly, beating thoroughly. Add lemon juice and continue beating until mixture is smooth and thick. Spoon filling into baked graham cracker crust. Top with cherry filling. Refrigerate several hours, or overnight, before serving.

## BLUEBERRY CHEESE PIE

1 9-inch pie

1 (8-ounce) package and 1
    (3-ounce) package cream
    cheese, softened
½ cup sugar
2 egg yolks

1½ teaspoons vanilla extract
1 (12-ounce) can SOLO Blueberry
    Filling
1 baked 9-inch pie shell

Blend together cream cheese, sugar, egg yolks, and vanilla. Beat until well blended and spoon into baked pie shell. Top with blueberry filling. Refrigerate several hours, or overnight, before serving.

## LEMON ANGEL PIE

1 8-inch pie

*A creamy sweet pie with a lovely tart flavor.*

2  egg whites
¼  teaspoon salt
    Pinch of cream of tartar
½  cup sugar

½  cup heavy cream
1  (12-ounce) can SOLO Lemon
    Filling

Preheat oven to 300° F. Lightly butter an 8-inch pie pan. Beat egg whites until foamy. Add salt and cream of tartar and continue beating until stiff but not dry. Gradually add sugar and continue beating until mixture is glossy. Spoon egg whites into pie pan, shaping mixture into shape of a pie shell. Bake 50 minutes. Remove from oven to cool thoroughly. (The egg white shell will rise and look gorgeous as it bakes, but it will fall in the center as it cools.) Whip cream just until cream stands in soft peaks. Add lemon filling and whip just until mixture is smooth. Pour mixture into shell and refrigerate until serving time.

## FRESH STRAWBERRY PIE

1 9-inch pie

2  pints fresh strawberries
1  (18-ounce) jar SOLO Strawberry
    Glaze

1  baked 9-inch pie shell
    Whipped cream

Wash, hull, and drain strawberries. Place in a mixing bowl and add glaze. Toss gently until strawberries are well coated with. glaze. Turn into baked pie shell. Refrigerate until chilled thoroughly. Top with whipped cream just before serving.

## BANANA-STRAWBERRY PIE

1 9-inch pie

2½  cups banana slices, cut
      ¼ inch thick (2 to 3 bananas)
1  (18-ounce) jar SOLO Strawberry
    Glaze

1  baked 9-inch graham cracker
    crust (see page 75)
    Whipped cream

Place banana slices in a mixing bowl. Add glaze and toss gently until slices are thoroughly coated. Turn into pie crust. Refrigerate until serving time, at least 1 hour. Garnish with whipped cream and extra banana slices.

*Opposite: Lemon Angel Pie and Fresh Strawberry Pie*

## SUPER PEACH PIE

1 9-inch pie

6 to 8 medium peaches
1 (18-ounce) jar SOLO Peach
   Glaze

1 baked 9-inch pie shell
Whipped cream

Place peaches in a bowl and pour boiling water over. Drain immediately and cover with cold water. Slip skins from peaches; cut into slices and place in a bowl. Add glaze and toss gently until slices are coated with glaze. Turn into pie shell. Refrigerate until chilled thoroughly. Serve topped with whipped cream.

## ALMOND CROWN PIE

1 9-inch pie

3 eggs
1 cup brown sugar, firmly
   packed
1 cup light corn syrup
1 teaspoon vanilla extract

½ (12-ounce) can SOLO Almond
   Filling
½ cup whole blanched almonds
1 unbaked 9-inch pie shell
½ cup slivered blanched almonds

Preheat oven to 350° F. Beat eggs and brown sugar together until thoroughly blended and foamy. Beat in corn syrup, vanilla, and almond filling. Form a crown inside pie shell by placing whole almonds on their sides around the edge. Carefully pour filling mixture into shell. Sprinkle with slivered almonds. Bake 1 hour, or until a knife inserted in center of pie comes out clean. Cool; refrigerate to chill thoroughly before cutting.

## CHOCOLATE ALMOND PIE

1 9-inch pie

*Chocolate and almond—great taste favorites—blended to make a delicious pie.*

3 (1-ounce) squares unsweetened
   chocolate
1 cup milk
½ cup sugar
6 tablespoons cornstarch
½ teaspoon salt
1 cup milk

3 eggs, separated
½ teaspoon vanilla extract
1 tablespoon butter or margarine
1 (12-ounce) can SOLO Almond
   Filling
6 tablespoons sugar
1 baked 9-inch pie shell

Bring water in bottom part of a double boiler to a boil. Combine chocolate and 1 cup milk in top part of double boiler and cook until chocolate is melted, stirring occasionally. In a bowl, combine ½ cup sugar, cornstarch, and salt and blend well. Stir in 1 cup milk. Add to chocolate mixture and cook over just boiling water, stirring occasionally, until mixture is very thick and smooth. Beat egg yolks lightly. Stir a little of the hot chocolate mixture into yolks and blend well. Return mixture to chocolate mixture in top part of double boiler and stir well to blend. Cook over hot water 2 to 3 minutes, stirring. Remove from heat and stir in vanilla, butter or margarine, and filling. Blend well. Cool. Beat egg whites until stiff. Gradually beat in 6 tablespoons sugar, 1 tablespoon at a time; continue beating until meringue is stiff and glossy. Preheat oven to 400° F. Pour chocolate mixture into baked pie shell. Top with meringue, making sure that meringue comes to the edge of crust and top of pie is well sealed. Bake 8 to 10 minutes, or until meringue is lightly browned. Remove from oven and cool thoroughly before serving.

**Good Idea: A wire whisk is perfect for blending any Solo filling into a mixture. It will break up the filling evenly so that the filling can be easily absorbed and blended.**

## CHOCOLATE ALMOND LAYER PIE                    1 9-inch pie

| | |
|---|---|
| 1 **(12-ounce) can SOLO Almond Filling** | ¼ **cup chopped toasted almonds** |
| 3 **tablespoons crème de cacao, brandy, or desired liqueur** | 3 **egg whites** |
| 1 **baked 9-inch pie shell** | 6 **tablespoons sugar** |
| 1 **pint chocolate ice cream, softened** | ½ **teaspoon vanilla extract** |

Combine almond filling and liqueur and blend well. Spread half of the filling in bottom of baked pie shell. Spread softened ice cream over filling. Top with remaining almond filling. Sprinkle chopped almonds over top. Freeze at least 6 to 8 hours or overnight. Preheat oven to 500° F. Beat egg whites just until stiff. Beat in sugar, one tablespoon at a time, and continue beating until mixture is stiff and glossy. Beat in vanilla. Spread meringue over top of pie, making sure that the meringue covers the crust of the pie and seals in the ice cream completely. Bake 3 to 5 minutes, or until meringue is lightly browned. Serve immediately or return to freezer until serving time.

## ALMOND SPONGE FLUFF PIE

1 9-inch pie

1 tablespoon (1 envelope)
   unflavored gelatine
3 eggs, separated
½ cup sugar
1 (12-ounce) can SOLO Almond
   Filling

¾ cup warm water
½ cup sugar
½ cup heavy cream
1 baked 9-inch pie shell

Soften gelatine in 2 tablespoons cold water. Beat egg yolks with ½ cup sugar in top part of a double broiler. Beat in almond filling. Stir in ¾ cup warm water. Cook over hot water, stirring occasionally, until mixture thickens. Remove from heat and stir in softened gelatine. Mix well and let cool until mixture starts to set. Beat egg whites until frothy. Gradually beat in ½ cup sugar and continue beating until stiff and glossy. Beat cream until stiff. Fold meringue and whipped cream into almond filling mixture. Pour into baked pie shell. Refrigerate for several hours, or until mixture is well set.

**Good Idea: When the meringue and whipped cream are blended into the almond mixture, let the mixture stand for a while in the bowl and stir often. When you turn the mixture into the pie shell, it will then mound up and make a beautiful pie.**

## RAISIN NUT PIE

1 9-inch pie

*This pie has a unique, very likable flavor that is hard to define unless you know how the pie is made.*

2 eggs, separated
¾ cup sugar
¼ teaspoon cinnamon
1 tablespoon melted butter or
   margarine

1 (10-ounce) jar SOLO Raisin
   Sauce
½ cup halved pecans
1 unbaked 9-inch pie shell

Preheat oven to 375° F. Beat egg yolks until fluffy and light in color. Beat in sugar, cinnamon, and butter or margarine. Stir in raisin sauce. Beat egg whites until stiff. Fold whites into egg yolk mixture together with pecans. Pour into pie shell. Bake 35 to 40 minutes, or until a silver knife inserted in center of pie comes out clean. Cool. Serve with a dab of whipped cream, if desired.

## APPLE-RAISIN CRUMB PIE

1 9-inch pie

*This is a fun pie with a very unusual flavor. The raisin sauce gives it a slightly pink color and a tart flavor and the topping adds crunchiness.*

4 to 5 apples, peeled, cored, and
    sliced (about 1 quart)
1 (10-ounce) jar SOLO Raisin
    Sauce
1 unbaked 9-inch pie shell
½ cup sugar
1 cup quick-cooking rolled oats

½ cup all-purpose flour
1 teaspoon cinnamon
½ teaspoon nutmeg
¼ teaspoon salt
½ cup butter or margarine,
    melted

Place apple slices in a saucepan with raisin sauce. Stew over medium heat about 10 minutes, stirring occasionally. Let stand a few minutes. Preheat oven to 450° F. Turn apple mixture into pie shell. Combine remaining ingredients and blend well. Sprinkle over top of apple mixture. Bake 10 minutes. Reduce heat to 350° F. and continue baking 40 to 45 minutes, or until crumbs are brown and crispy. Cool before cutting.

**Good Idea: The kind of apples used in this pie will determine the cooking time. A tart, crisp apple should cook about 10 minutes. If the apple is mild in flavor and soft, cook it a shorter length of time. The apple slices should not turn into mush.**

## COCONUT CRUNCH PIE

1 9-inch pie

*This crunchy pie looks like a lemon pie, tastes a little like custard, and is a pleasant surprise.*

3 eggs, separated
1¼ cups sugar
1 teaspoon salt
½ cup milk
2 tablespoons butter or
    margarine, melted

¼ teaspoon lemon extract
½ teaspoon almond extract
1 cup SOLO Coconut Flake
1 unbaked 9-inch pie shell

Preheat oven to 350° F. Beat egg yolks thoroughly. Beat in sugar and salt and mix well. Stir in milk, butter or margarine, and extracts. Fold in coconut. Beat egg whites until stiff but not dry. Fold into yolk mixture. Pour into pie shell. Bake 45 to 50 minutes, or until a silver knife inserted in center of pie comes out clean.

## SOUR CREAM PRUNE PIE

1 8-inch pie

*This pie, with an unusual tart-sweet flavor, will become a favorite of the whole family.*

½ cup sugar
½ teaspoon ground cloves
½ teaspoon cinnamon
¼ teaspoon salt
2 eggs, well beaten

1 (12-ounce) can SOLO Prune Filling
1 cup dairy sour cream
1 unbaked 8-inch pie shell

Preheat oven to 350° F. Combine sugar, cloves, cinnamon, and salt. Add to eggs and blend well. Beat in filling and sour cream. Pour into pie shell. Bake 50 to 60 minutes, or just until a silver knife inserted in center of pie comes out clean. Remove from oven and cool before serving.

## PRUNE WHIP PIE

1 9-inch pie

4 egg whites
½ cup sugar
1½ teaspoons lemon juice
⅛ teaspoon salt
1 (12-ounce) can SOLO Prune Filling

1 baked 9-inch pie shell
1 cup heavy cream, whipped
Cinnamon
SOLO Coconut Flake

Preheat oven to 325° F. Beat egg whites until stiff. Gradually add sugar and continue beating until stiff and glossy. Fold in lemon juice, salt, and prune filling. Spoon into baked pie shell. Bake 15 minutes. Cool. Top with whipped cream and a sprinkle of cinnamon and coconut.

## COTTAGE PRUNE PIE

1 9-inch pie

1 (12-ounce) can SOLO Prune
    Filling
1 unbaked 9-inch pie shell
2 eggs, lightly beaten
½ cup sugar

½ teaspoon salt
1 cup creamy cottage cheese
¼ cup milk
½ cup light cream
1 teaspoon cinnamon

Preheat oven to 450° F. Spread prune filling on bottom of unbaked pie shell. Combine eggs, sugar, and salt. Add cottage cheese, milk, and cream and blend well. Spoon mixture over prune filling. Sprinkle with cinnamon. Bake 10 minutes. Reduce temperature to 325° F. and continue baking 55 to 60 minutes, or until a silver knife inserted in center of pie comes out clean. Cool well before serving.

♫ Good Idea: If you find this pie too sweet for your taste, use a little less sugar the next time you make it.

## DATE CUSTARD PIE

1 9-inch pie

4 eggs
⅓ cup sugar
½ teaspoon salt
¼ teaspoon nutmeg
1 (12-ounce) can SOLO Date
    Filling

½ teaspoon vanilla extract
2 cups milk
1 unbaked 9-inch sesame pie
    shell (see page 75)
6 tablespoons sugar

Preheat oven to 450° F. Separate 3 eggs. Add 1 whole egg to yolks and beat well. Add ⅓ cup sugar, salt, and nutmeg and beat well. Beat in filling until mixture is well blended. Stir in vanilla and milk. Turn mixture into pie shell. Bake 10 minutes. Reduce heat to 350° F. and bake 50 to 60 minutes, or until pie is almost set. Remove pie from oven. Beat 3 egg whites until stiff. Add 6 tablespoons sugar, 1 tablespoonful at a time, beating well after each addition. Continue beating until stiff and glossy. Swirl meringue over top of date filling. Be sure that meringue comes up to crust, and top of pie is sealed in. Bake about 15 minutes, or until meringue is lightly browned. Remove and cool before serving.

♫ Good Idea: When topping a pie with a meringue, be sure that it comes up to the crust all the way around and that it touches the crust. Also, be sure that the top of the pie is completely sealed in; otherwise the meringue will shrink from the crust and make a less-than-attractive top.

## LITTLE CHESS PIES

12 tarts

½  cup butter or margarine
1  teaspoon vanilla extract
1  cup sugar
1  (11½-ounce) can SOLO Nut
    Filling

3  eggs
1  cup chopped seedless raisins
12  unbaked 3-inch tart shells

Preheat oven to 400° F. Cream butter or margarine and vanilla together. Add sugar and beat until fluffy. Add nut filling and beat until well blended. Add eggs, one at a time, beating well after each addition. Stir in raisins. Divide mixture among unbaked tart shells. Bake 25 to 30 minutes, or until a silver knife inserted in center of tart comes out clean. Cool before serving. Serve with a dab of whipped cream, if desired.

🎵 **Good Idea: If you do not have 3-inch tart or muffin pans, these tarts can, of course, be made smaller. Fill tart shells almost to the top; bake about 25 minutes and test with a knife for doneness.**

86

## SOLO MINI TARTS

about 2½ dozen

1  (3-ounce) package cream
    cheese, softened
½  cup butter or margarine

1  cup all-purpose flour
1  (12-ounce) can SOLO filling,
    any desired flavor

Preheat oven to 400° F. Combine cream cheese and butter or margarine and blend well. Add flour and blend well. Shape dough into 1-inch balls and place in 1¾-inch muffin pan cups. Press dough with fingers to cover sides and bottom of each cup. Bake 15 minutes, or until lightly browned and done. Cool shells in pan. When cool, remove from pans and fill with desired flavor of filling. Top with a dollop of flavored whipped cream, if desired.

🎵 **Good Idea: In these tarts, try using a variety of leftover fillings, or fill with fresh fruit and top with your choice of Solo glaze.**

*Opposite: Solo Mini Tarts*

## SOLO POPPY CUSTARD PIE

1 9-inch pie

4 eggs
⅓ cup sugar
1 tablespoon grated lemon peel
1 (12-ounce) can SOLO Poppy
    Filling

½ cup frozen orange juice
    concentrate, undiluted
1½ cups milk
1 unbaked 9-inch pie shell
6 tablespoons sugar

Preheat oven to 450° F. Separate 3 eggs. Add 1 whole egg to yolks and beat well. Add ⅓ cup sugar and lemon peel. Add poppy filling and blend well. Stir in orange juice concentrate and milk and blend. Spoon mixture into unbaked pie shell. Bake 10 minutes. Reduce heat to 350° F. and bake 50 to 60 minutes, or until pie is almost set. Beat egg whites until stiff. Add 6 tablespoons sugar, 1 tablespoonful at a time, beating well after each addition. Continue beating until stiff and glossy. Swirl meringue over hot poppy pie, making sure that meringue comes up to crust, sealing in entire top of pie. Bake about 15 minutes, or until meringue is lightly browned. Remove and cool before serving.

## FROZEN LEMON VELVET PIE

1 9-inch pie

1¼ cups fine vanilla wafer
    crumbs
6 tablespoons butter or
    margarine, melted
1 (8-ounce) package cream
    cheese, softened

1 cup heavy cream
¼ cup sugar
½ teaspoon vanilla extract
1 (12-ounce) can SOLO Lemon
    Filling

Combine crumbs and melted butter or margarine; blend well. Press firmly onto bottom and sides of a buttered 9-inch pie plate. Refrigerate until firm. Beat cream cheese until fluffy. In a separate bowl, beat cream until thickened but not stiff. Gradually add whipped cream to the whipped cheese, beating until smooth and creamy. Beat in sugar and vanilla. Fold in lemon filling. Spoon mixture into chilled pie crust and freeze until firm. Remove from freezer about 10 minutes before serving.

## STRAWBERRY PARFAIT PIE

1 9-inch pie

1 (3-ounce) package strawberry-
    flavored gelatin
1¼ cups boiling water
1 pint vanilla ice cream,
    softened

1 cup thawed and drained frozen
    strawberries
1 baked 9-inch pie shell
1 cup SOLO Strawberry Glaze

Dissolve gelatin in boiling water. Add ice cream and stir until melted. Refrigerate until thick but not set, about 20 minutes. Fold in strawberries. Pour half of the mixture into pie shell and refrigerate until firm. Spread glaze evenly over mixture. Pour remaining strawberry mixture over top of glaze. Refrigerate until firm.

**Good Idea: Substitute frozen blueberries and blueberry glaze for a delicious variation on this parfait pie.**

## ICE CREAM PIE

1 9-inch pie

1½ cups cinnamon graham cracker
    crumbs
⅓ cup sugar
½ cup melted butter or margarine

1 quart vanilla ice cream
1 (12-ounce) can SOLO Pineapple
    Filling

Combine cracker crumbs, sugar, and butter or margarine. Blend well. Press into a 9-inch pie pan and refrigerate 45 minutes. Stir ice cream to soften. Blend in pineapple filling and mix well. Pour into chilled crumb crust. Place in freezer for at least 4 hours, or until very firm. Remove from freezer and let stand 5 to 10 minutes before cutting.

**Good Idea: If cinnamon graham crackers are not available in your market, add ½ teaspoon ground cinnamon to 1½ cups of crumbs made with regular graham crackers.**

# The Cake Box

**PRUNE DREAM CAKE**                                1 8-inch cake

2 cups all-purpose flour
1¼ cups sugar
2½ teaspoons double-acting
    baking powder
½ teaspoon baking soda
½ teaspoon salt

½ cup soft margarine or
    shortening
2 eggs
1 (12-ounce) can SOLO Prune
    Filling
1 teaspoon vanilla extract

Preheat oven to 375° F. Grease, then line with a circle of waxed paper, and grease again two 8-inch round cake pans. Put the flour, sugar, baking powder, baking soda, and salt in the large bowl of an electric mixer. Stir lightly. Add margarine or shortening, eggs, and half of the prune filling. With electric mixer on low, blend mixture. When well blended, beat at medium speed about 2 minutes. Add remaining prune filling and vanilla. Beat 1 minute, or until mixture is blended. Divide batter between prepared pans. Bake 25 minutes, or until a cake tester inserted in center of cake comes out clean. Remove from oven and let stand on wire rack 5 minutes. Remove cake from pan and remove waxed paper. Let stand until cold. Fill and frost cake with Butter Cream Frosting (see page 108).

## SOUR CREAM-PECAN CAKE

9 servings

⅓ cup butter or margarine
1 cup sugar
2 eggs
2 cups all-purpose flour
1½ teaspoons baking powder

½ teaspoon baking soda
½ teaspoon salt
1 cup dairy sour cream
1 (11½-ounce) can SOLO Pecan
    Filling

Preheat oven to 350° F. Butter and lightly flour a 9-inch-square pan. Cream butter or margarine and sugar together until light and fluffy. Add eggs, one at a time, beating well after each addition. Sift together flour, baking powder, baking soda, and salt. Add to creamed mixture alternately with sour cream, beginning and ending with dry ingredients. Spread batter in prepared pan. Drop pecan filling by spoonfuls on top of cake batter. Swirl lightly through batter with a knife. Bake 45 to 50 minutes, or until a cake tester inserted in center of cake comes out clean. Let cool in pan before cutting into serving pieces.

♪ **Good Idea:** You can use only ½ can of the Solo Pecan Filling, saving the rest for another recipe. The cake this way is equally good.

91

## TOPSY-TURVY CAKE

9 servings

1 (12-ounce) can SOLO Apricot
    Filling
½ cup SOLO Coconut Flake
2 tablespoons melted butter or
    margarine
1⅓ cups all-purpose flour
⅔ cup sugar

2 teaspoons baking powder
½ teaspoon salt
2 eggs, well beaten
½ cup milk
¼ cup melted butter or margarine
1 teaspoon vanilla extract

Preheat oven to 350° F. Combine apricot filling, coconut flake, and 2 tablespoons melted butter or margarine. Spread in bottom of a 9-inch layer cake pan. Set aside. Sift together flour, sugar, baking powder, and salt. Beat together eggs, milk, ¼ cup melted butter or margarine, and vanilla. Add to dry ingredients and stir just until mixture is smooth. Pour over apricot mixture in pan. Bake 20 to 25 minutes, or until a cake tester inserted in center of cake comes out clean. Let cake stand on wire rack 2 to 3 minutes. Invert onto serving plate and let stand a few minutes. Remove cake pan and remove any bits of filling still in pan and spread on cake. Serve warm with whipped cream, if desired.

## TORTE SUPREME

14 to 16 servings

1¾ cups all-purpose flour
½ cup sugar
½ teaspoon baking powder
5 eggs, separated
1 cup butter or margarine
3 tablespoons milk
1 teaspoon grated lemon peel

1 teaspoon vanilla extract
1 (12-ounce) can SOLO
   Raspberry Filling
1 cup sugar
1 cup SOLO Coconut Flake
1½ cups heavy cream

Preheat oven to 350° F. Grease three 9-inch layer cake pans. Into a large bowl, measure flour, ½ cup sugar, baking powder, egg yolks, butter or margarine, milk, lemon peel, and vanilla. Beat with mixer at low speed just until mixed; increase speed to high and beat 4 minutes, scraping bowl occasionally. Divide batter among pans; spread top of each layer with one-quarter can raspberry filling. Beat egg whites at high speed until soft peaks form. Gradually sprinkle in 1 cup sugar, 2 tablespoons at a time. Continue beating at high speed until sugar is completely dissolved and egg whites stand in stiff peaks. Gently fold in coconut. Spread one-third of the mixture over each layer. Bake 30 to 35 minutes, or until golden. Cool in pans on wire rack 15 minutes. Remove from pans and finish cooling. Whip cream until stiff. Put layers together with whipped cream and garnish top with remaining raspberry filling.

## ALMOND CAKE

1 10-inch tube cake

1 cup butter or margarine
1 cup sugar
3 eggs
1 (12-ounce) can SOLO Almond
   Filling

2¼ cups all-purpose flour
2 teaspoons baking powder
½ teaspoon salt
¼ cup milk
Almond Glaze (recipe follows)

Preheat oven to 350° F. Grease and lightly flour a 10-inch tube or bundt pan. Cream butter or margarine and sugar together until light and fluffy. Add eggs, one at a time, mixing thoroughly after each addition. Beat in almond filling. Sift together flour, baking powder, and salt. Add to creamed mixture alternately with the milk, beginning and ending with dry ingredients. Blend thoroughly. Turn batter into prepared pan. Bake 50 minutes, or until a cake tester inserted in center of cake comes out clean. Cool about 10 minutes. Remove from pan and cool thoroughly. Serve plain or frost with Almond Glaze.

## Almond Glaze

1 cup confectioners sugar      ¼ teaspoon almond extract
2 tablespoons light cream

Combine all ingredients and stir until well blended and smooth. Drizzle over top of Almond Cake.

## ALMOND JOY CAKE

2½ cups all-purpose flour
1 teaspoon baking powder
½ teaspoon salt
2 cups sugar
1 cup soft shortening or
     softened margarine

¾ cup milk
2 eggs
1 (12-ounce) can SOLO Almond
     Filling
2 cups whipped topping

Preheat oven to 375° F. Grease and line the bottoms of two 9-inch layer cake pans with waxed paper and grease again. Sift together flour, baking powder, and salt in large bowl of electric mixer. Stir in sugar. Add shortening or margarine, milk, eggs, and almond filling. Beat at low speed until blended. Beat at medium speed 3 to 4 minutes, or until batter is smooth and thick. Divide batter between prepared pans. Bake 30 to 35 minutes, or until a cake tester inserted in center of cake comes out clean. Let stand on cooling rack 5 minutes. Turn out of pans to cool thoroughly. Spread topping between layers and over top of cake.

93

**Good idea: This is a moist, chewy cake with a definite almond flavor. Instead of frosting with topping, the cake can be cut into individual servings and topped with a spoonful of flavored whipped cream. When peaches are in season, top each serving with a few slices of sweetened fresh peaches for a memorable flavor.**

## SOLO POPPY CAKE

1 10-inch tube cake

*The delicious, delicate flavor of this innovative cake is reminiscent of a spice cake and it stays fresh for a very long time!*

| | |
|---|---|
| 1 cup butter or margarine, softened | 1 teaspoon vanilla extract |
| | 1 cup dairy sour cream |
| 1½ cups sugar | 2½ cups all-purpose flour |
| 1 (12-ounce) can SOLO Poppy Filling | 1 teaspoon baking soda |
| | 1 teaspoon salt |
| 4 eggs, separated | Confectioners sugar |

Preheat oven to 350° F. Grease and lightly flour a 9- or 10-inch tube pan. Cream butter or margarine and sugar together until light and fluffy. Add poppy filling. Add egg yolks, one at a time, beating well after each addition. Add vanilla and sour cream. Sift together flour, baking soda, and salt; add to mixture gradually, beating well after each addition. Beat egg whites until stiff but not dry; fold into batter. Turn batter into prepared pan. Bake about 1 hour and 10 to 15 minutes, or until a cake tester inserted in center of cake comes out clean. Allow cake to cool about 5 minutes. Remove from pan. To decorate, sift confectioners sugar through a paper doily or a cutout on the top of the cake.

94

 **Good Idea: If you prefer, bake two 9-inch round layers and reduce baking time to 45 minutes, or until done. Cool layers and put together with a cream filling.**

*Opposite: Solo Poppy Cake*

## QUICK LEMON BUNDT CAKE

1 10-inch tube cake

1 (1-pound 2½-ounce) package
   yellow cake mix
1 (3½-ounce) package lemon
   instant pudding mix

4 eggs
½ cup cooking oil
1 (12-ounce) can SOLO Lemon
   Filling

Preheat oven to 350° F. Grease and lightly flour a 10-inch tube or bundt pan. Place all ingredients into the large bowl of an electric mixer. Mix at low speed until all ingredients are blended, using a rubber scraper to push ingredients into mixer blades. Beat at medium speed about 3 minutes, or until well blended and smooth. Do not overbeat. Turn batter into prepared pan. Bake 60 to 70 minutes, or until a cake tester inserted in center of cake comes out clean. Let stand in pan about 5 minutes. Turn out of pan onto a wire rack and let stand until thoroughly cool before cutting.

## CHOCOLATE ALMOND CAKE

1 10-inch tube cake

1 (1-pound 2½-ounce) package
   chocolate cake mix
1 (3½-ounce) package chocolate
   instant pudding mix

4 eggs
½ cup cooking oil
1 (12-ounce) can SOLO Almond
   Filling

Make and bake as above.

## RASPBERRY CAKE

1 10-inch tube cake

1 (1-pound 2½-ounce) package
   yellow cake mix
1 (3½-ounce) package vanilla
   instant pudding mix
4 eggs

½ cup cooking oil
1 (12-ounce) can SOLO Raspberry
   Filling
2 tablespoons brandy

Make and bake as above.

♫ Good Idea: Use any Solo fruit filling in place of the raspberry for a simple yet delicious variation.

## RASPBERRY ANGEL CAKE

1 loaf cake

1 (3-ounce) package raspberry-
  flavored gelatin
1 cup boiling water
1 (12-ounce) can SOLO Raspberry
  Filling

1 angel food or sponge loaf
  cake (9 x 5 x 3 inches)
1 cup heavy cream
1 tablespoon brandy
¼ cup SOLO Coconut Flake

In a mixing bowl, combine gelatin and boiling water and stir until gelatin is dissolved. Refrigerate until mixture is slightly syrupy. Stir in raspberry filling and blend thoroughly. Refrigerate until mixture mounds from a spoon. Cut angel cake into 3 layers horizontally. Spread half the gelatin mixture on bottom layer. Top with second layer and top with remaining gelatin mixture. Place top on cake. Refrigerate until gelatin is thoroughly set. Whip cream until stiff. Fold in brandy. Spread on top and sides of cake. Sprinkle with coconut. Refrigerate until serving time.

**Good Idea: Place bottom layer of cake on an oblong platter or plate with some lip before placing gelatin mixture on cake. To keep layers from sliding during chilling, place 2 or 3 food picks through layers. Remove before frosting with cream.**

## PINEAPPLE ICE CREAM ANGEL CAKE

12 to 14 servings

1 10-inch angel food cake
1 quart vanilla ice cream,
  slightly softened
1 (12-ounce) can SOLO Pineapple
  Filling

1 cup heavy cream
2 tablespoons sugar
1 teaspoon vanilla extract
  SOLO Coconut Flake

Turn cake upside down and carefully slice 1 inch from bottom of cake. Using a fork, carefully dig out center of cake, leaving a 1-inch wall around outer edge, inner ring, and top of cake. (You can later fill the tube hole with the cake pieces or reserve them for use in another dessert.) Place cake upside down on a serving plate. Blend ice cream and pineapple filling together and spoon into scooped-out portion of cake. Replace bottom of cake. Beat cream until stiff. Beat in sugar and vanilla. Spread quickly over top and sides of cake. Place cake in freezer and freeze about 4 hours, or until very firm. Remove from freezer and sprinkle with coconut. Let stand about 10 minutes before serving.

**Good Idea: If this cake proves difficult to serve, use a serrated knife, dipping it into hot water after every few slices.**

## PINEAPPLE UPSIDE-DOWN CAKE

9 servings

3 tablespoons butter or margarine
1 (12-ounce) can SOLO Pineapple Filling
½ cup butter or margarine, softened

½ cup sugar
1 egg
1½ cups all-purpose flour
1½ teaspoons baking powder
½ teaspoon salt
½ cup milk

Preheat oven to 375° F. Melt 3 tablespoons butter or margarine in a 9-inch-square pan. Spread pineapple filling over butter. Cream ½ cup butter or margarine and sugar together until light and fluffy. Beat in egg. Sift together flour, baking powder, and salt. Add to creamed mixture alternately with milk, beginning and ending with dry ingredients. Spoon batter carefully over top of pineapple. Smooth out. Bake about 35 minutes, or until a cake tester inserted in center of cake comes out clean. Let stand in pan 5 minutes. Turn cake out on serving plate. Scrape out remaining pineapple in pan and smooth over top of cake. Serve warm with sweetened whipped cream or ice cream, if desired.

## MARTHA WASHINGTON CHERRY TORTE

1 9-inch cake

3 eggs, separated
⅓ cup water
1 teaspoon grated lemon peel
½ teaspoon vanilla extract
1 cup sugar
2 tablespoons lemon juice
1¼ cups sifted cake flour

1 teaspoon baking powder
½ teaspoon salt
1 (3-ounce) package vanilla pudding and pie filling mix
2 cups milk
1 (12-ounce) can SOLO Cherry Filling

Preheat oven to 375° F. Grease two 9-inch layer cake pans and line with a circle of waxed paper; grease again. Combine egg yolks, water, lemon peel, and vanilla in a mixing bowl. Beat with rotary beater until light in color. Add sugar and lemon juice; beat well. Sift together flour, baking powder, and salt. Fold dry ingredients into egg yolk mixture and stir just enough to make a smooth batter. Beat egg whites until stiff but not dry. Fold into batter. Pour into prepared pans. Bake 12 to 15 minutes, or until cake springs back when lightly touched with fingers. Cool in pans about 5 minutes. Turn out of pans, remove paper, and cool thoroughly. Prepare pudding mix, using 2 cups milk. Cool. Spread pudding between two layers of cake. Top cake with cherry filling. Serve with whipped cream, if desired.

*Opposite: Martha Washington Cherry Torte*

## SPITZER'S TORTE

12 to 14 servings

1 (12-ounce) can SOLO Cherry
   Filling
¼ cup brandy
1 (1-pound 2½-ounce) package
   chocolate cake mix

2 tablespoons sugar
1 cup heavy cream

Combine cherry filling and brandy. Set aside. Prepare cake mix according to package directions, baking in two 9-inch layer cake pans. Cool. Whip cream until stiff. Beat in sugar and additional brandy (if desired). Spread half the cherry filling over one cake layer and top with part of the whipped cream. Put second layer on top. Top with remaining cherry filling. Frost top and sides with remaining whipped cream. Refrigerate to chill cake thoroughly before serving.

## SOLO CHERRY POLKA DOT CAKE

9 servings

⅓ cup butter or margarine
1 cup sugar
1 egg
½ teaspoon vanilla extract
1⅔ cups all-purpose flour
½ teaspoon baking powder
½ teaspoon baking soda

½ teaspoon salt
¾ cup water
1 (12-ounce) can SOLO Cherry
   Filling
2 tablespoons brandy
½ cup toasted sliced almonds

Preheat oven to 350° F. Grease and lightly flour a 9-inch-square baking pan. Cream butter or margarine and sugar together until light and fluffy. Add egg and vanilla and beat well. Sift together flour, baking powder, baking soda, and salt. Add to creamed mixture alternately with water, beginning and ending with dry ingredients and blending well after each addition. Stir in 2 tablespoons cherry filling. Turn batter into prepared pan. Bake 30 to 35 minutes, or until a cake tester inserted in center of cake comes out clean. Remove from oven and cool on rack. Combine remaining cherry filling and brandy. Spread over cake while it is still warm. Sprinkle top with almonds. Serve warm or cold.

♫ **Good Idea: With both cherry in the cake and cherry on the top and with the addition of brandy, this cake is quite festive. If served warm, you might add a dollop of whipped cream to which has been added brandy instead of vanilla for flavoring.**

# MELBA CHEESECAKE

12 to 16 servings

1⅔ cups graham cracker crumbs
(18 crackers)

⅓ cup butter or margarine,
melted

⅛ teaspoon cinnamon

⅛ teaspoon nutmeg

3 large eggs
Sugar

3 (8-ounce) packages cream
cheese, softened
Vanilla extract

2 cups dairy sour cream

1 (12-ounce) can SOLO Cherry,
Strawberry, or Blueberry
Filling

Preheat oven to 350° F. Oil the bottom of a 9-inch springform pan. Place crackers in a plastic bag and crush with a rolling pin. Pour into a bowl. Add butter or margarine, cinnamon, and nutmeg; blend thoroughly. Press firmly on bottom of springform pan. Beat eggs with mixer at low speed until well blended. Gradually add ¾ cup sugar and beat until thickened. Cut cream cheese into chunks and add gradually to egg mixture. Continue beating until mixture is very smooth. Add 1 teaspoon vanilla. Pour mixture into springform pan. Bake 45 minutes, or until cake is fairly firm. Remove cake from oven. Turn temperature up to 450° F. Combine sour cream, ⅓ cup sugar, and 1 teaspoon vanilla. Spread gently over top of cheesecake. Bake 4 to 5 minutes, or just until topping is set. Remove from oven and cool. Refrigerate overnight. Before serving, spread top with desired fruit filling.

Good Idea: To vary the recipe, top the cake with fresh fruit before serving and cover with Solo fruit glaze.

## APRICOT CHEESECAKE

12 to 16 servings

*A special cheesecake that even those who don't care for cheesecake love. Apricot gives it a pleasant tasting bite.*

1⅔ cups graham cracker crumbs
    (18 crackers)

¼ cup sugar

⅓ cup butter or margarine,
    melted

1 (8-ounce) package and 1
    (3-ounce) package cream
    cheese, softened

2 eggs, separated

½ cup sugar

1 (12-ounce) can SOLO Apricot
    Filling

½ teaspoon vanilla extract

1 cup dairy sour cream

Place crackers in a plastic bag and crush with a rolling pin. Combine with ¼ cup sugar and butter or margarine. Blend well. Press mixture onto bottom and partway up sides of a 9-inch springform pan. Set prepared pan aside. Preheat oven to 325° F. Combine cream cheese, egg yolks, and ½ cup sugar. Beat until well blended and fluffy. Add apricot filling and vanilla and blend well. Beat egg whites until stiff but not dry. Fold into cream cheese mixture. Pour mixture into prepared pan. Bake 1 hour and 10 minutes, or just until set. Remove from oven and very carefully spread sour cream over top of cake. Return to oven and bake 5 minutes longer. Remove from oven and cool thoroughly before serving.

## APRICOT CAKE
## "THROUGH AND THROUGH"

12 to 14 servings

½ cup butter or margarine

1¼ cups sugar

2 eggs

2 teaspoons grated lemon peel

1 (12-ounce) can SOLO Apricot
    Filling

2 cups all-purpose flour

3 teaspoons baking powder

¼ teaspoon baking soda

1 teaspoon salt

1 cup milk

Preheat oven to 350° F. Grease a 13- x 9- x 2-inch baking pan. Cream butter or margarine and sugar together until light and fluffy. Add eggs, one at a time, beating well after each addition. Stir in lemon peel and ⅓ cup of the apricot filling. Sift together flour, baking powder, baking soda, and salt. Add to creamed mixture alternately with milk, beginning and ending with dry ingredients. Pour batter into prepared pan and smooth top lightly. Bake 35 to 40 minutes, or until a cake tester inserted in center of cake comes out clean. Cool in pan about 10 minutes. Spread remaining apricot filling on top of cake. Cut into squares and serve warm or cold with a topping of whipped cream, if desired.

## APRICOT CRUMB CAKE

12 to 16 servings

½ cup butter or margarine, softened

1 (8-ounce) package cream cheese, softened

1¼ cups sugar

1 teaspoon vanilla extract

2 eggs

2 cups sifted cake flour

1 teaspoon baking powder

½ teaspoon baking soda

¼ teaspoon salt

¼ cup milk

1 (12-ounce) can SOLO Apricot Filling

2 cups SOLO Coconut Flake

⅔ cup brown sugar, firmly packed

1 teaspoon cinnamon

⅓ cup butter or margarine, melted

Preheat oven to 350° F. Cream softened butter or margarine, cream cheese, and sugar together until light and fluffy. Add vanilla and eggs and beat thoroughly. Combine cake flour, baking powder, baking soda, and salt. Add to creamed mixture, alternating with milk, beginning and ending with dry ingredients. Grease and lightly flour a 13- x 9- x 2-inch baking pan. Spread half the batter in bottom of pan; spoon apricot filling on top; cover with remaining batter. Bake 40 minutes. Combine coconut, brown sugar, cinnamon, and melted butter or margarine; sprinkle over cake. Place cake under broiler until topping is golden brown.

103

♫ Good Idea: For an attractive variation, bake the cake in a quiche pan.

## HAWAIIAN DELIGHT PINEAPPLE CAKE

1 8-inch cake

1 (9-ounce) package white cake
  mix
3 tablespoons brown sugar
1 tablespoon butter or margarine

1 cup SOLO Coconut Flake
½ (12-ounce) can SOLO Pineapple
  Filling

Prepare cake according to package directions, baking in an 8-inch-square cake pan. When cake is baked, remove from oven and cool 5 minutes. Preheat broiler. Combine remaining ingredients, blending well. Spread over top of cake, making sure to cover entire top of cake up to edge of pan. Broil, about 4 inches from source of heat, until delicately brown and bubbly. Cool and cut into squares before serving. Serve with whipped cream, if desired.

## DATE NUT CAKE

9 servings

1 (12-ounce) can SOLO Date
  Filling
½ cup water
¼ cup butter or margarine
1 cup sugar
1 teaspoon vanilla extract

1 egg
1⅔ cups all-purpose flour
1 teaspoon baking soda
½ teaspoon salt
½ cup chopped walnuts

Preheat oven to 350° F. Grease and lightly flour a 9-inch-square baking pan. Combine date filling and water and set aside. Cream butter or margarine, sugar, and vanilla together until light and fluffy. Beat in egg. Sift together flour, baking soda, and salt. Add dry ingredients to creamed mixture alternately with date-water mixture, beginning and ending with dry ingredients. Blend until smooth. Stir in nuts. Pour into prepared pan. Bake 50 to 60 minutes, or until a cake tester inserted in center of cake comes out clean. Let cake stand in pan to cool. Cut into squares and serve plain or frosted with whipped cream, if desired.

♫ **Good Idea: This cake freezes beautifully, can be defrosted and refrozen again. And, wrapped in plastic wrap, it will stay fresh and lovely for days on the shelf at room temperature—perfect for neighbors who drop in unexpectedly!**

*Opposite: Hawaiian Delight Pineapple Cake and Date Nut Cake*

## BUTTER CREAM POUND CAKE

1 10-inch tube cake

1 pound confectioners sugar
1 pound butter or margarine,
   softened
1 teaspoon vanilla extract
6 eggs

4 cups all-purpose flour
2 teaspoons baking powder
1 (12-ounce) can SOLO Poppy
   Filling

Preheat oven to 325° F. Grease and lightly flour a 10-inch tube or bundt pan. Cream the confectioners sugar, butter or margarine, and vanilla together at medium speed of an electric mixer until mixture is very fluffy. Add eggs, one at a time, beating well after each addition. Scrape bottom and sides of bowl often during mixing time with a rubber scraper. Sift together flour and baking powder. Gradually beat into batter, until mixture is very smooth, scraping bottom and sides of bowl with scraper. Remove about 3 cups of the batter and add the poppy filling to it. Blend thoroughly. Spread half of remaining plain batter over bottom of prepared pan. Add alternate spoonfuls of the poppy seed and plain batter until both batters are all in the pan. Smooth out top of batter. Bake 1 hour and 30 minutes, or until a cake tester inserted in center of cake comes out clean. Remove from oven and let stand in pan about 10 minutes. Invert out of pan onto a wire rack and cool thoroughly before cutting. Sprinkle with confectioners sugar or frost with a glaze made of confectioners sugar and lemon juice, if desired.

## SOLO FROSTED CUPCAKES

Cut cone shape from top of cupcake and remove. Fill hole with desired fruit filling. Replace cone whole or butterflied. For variety, frost cupcakes with any of the following frostings and sprinkle with Solo Coconut Flake, if desired.

## SOLO FLUFFY FRUIT FROSTING

about 2 cups

½ cup SOLO Pineapple Filling
½ cup SOLO Apricot Filling

1 cup heavy cream, whipped
   Slivered toasted almonds

Combine pineapple and apricot fillings. Fold into whipped cream. Use to frost angel food or plain cake. Sprinkle slivered almonds over top. Serve cake immediately.

*Opposite: Solo Frosted Cupcakes*

## SOLO BROILER FRUIT FROSTING

about 2½ cups

*An old-fashioned frosting—like mother used to make—that's a modern-day time-saver.*

2 tablespoons butter or
    margarine
5 tablespoons brown sugar
1 cup SOLO Coconut Flake

1 (12-ounce) can SOLO Date,
    Pineapple, or other fruit
    filling

Cream butter or margarine and brown sugar together. Blend in coconut and filling. Spread over top of flat cake either 13 x 9 x 3 inches or 9 inches square. (Frosting will be thinner on larger cake, but will be enough to cover.) Place under broiler and broil until delicately browned. Watch carefully for last few minutes so that frosting does not burn. Cool. Cut into squares and serve.

## 3 MINUTE SOLO DATE FROSTING

about 1½ cups

2 egg whites
3 tablespoons water
¼ teaspoon cream of tartar

1 cup sugar
⅓ cup SOLO Date Filling

Put enough water in the bottom of a double boiler to fill it completely when the top section is put in place. Cover and heat water to boiling. In top of double boiler, combine egg whites, water, cream of tartar, and sugar. Mix well. Remove boiling water from heat. Put top of double boiler into bottom of double boiler. Beat egg white mixture with a rotary beater or electric mixer for 3 minutes. Stir in date filling.

♫**Good Idea: This is especially tasty on yellow or spice cakes.**

## SOLO BUTTER CREAM FROSTING

about 2 cups

¼ cup softened butter or
    margarine
2 cups sifted confectioners
    sugar

¼ cup SOLO Pineapple or Apricot
    Filling
1 teaspoon grated orange peel

Cream butter or margarine. Beat in sugar, alternately with filling, until mixture is smooth and creamy. Add orange peel.

## SOLO WHIPPED CREAM TOPPING

about 2 cups

1 (12-ounce) can SOLO Date or
   Prune Filling

1 cup heavy cream, whipped

Fold filling into whipped cream. Spoon topping over warm gingerbread or spice cake.

## SOLO FRUIT ROLL

about 10 servings

3 large eggs
1 cup sugar
⅓ cup water
1 teaspoon vanilla extract
1 cup sifted cake flour

1 teaspoon baking powder
¼ teaspoon salt
   Confectioners sugar
1 (12-ounce) can SOLO Raspberry
   or Strawberry Filling

Preheat oven to 375° F. Grease a 15- x 10- x 1-inch jelly roll pan. Line with brown paper or aluminum foil and grease again. In small bowl of electric mixer beat eggs until thick and lemon-colored. Pour eggs into large bowl. Gradually beat in sugar and continue beating until well blended. Beat in water and vanilla. Sift together flour, baking powder, and salt. Carefully fold into egg mixture with a rubber scraper. Pour into prepared pan. Bake 12 to 15 minutes, or until cake springs back when touched lightly with finger. Sprinkle a towel with confectioners sugar. As soon as cake is done, loosen edges from pan and turn pan upside down on towel. Carefully peel off paper. Trim off any hard or stiff edges of cake. While cake is hot, roll up cake and towel together from one end. Wrap in another towel and let stand until cool. Unroll cake and remove towel. Spread with filling and roll up again. Sprinkle top with additional confectioners sugar. Cut into 1-inch slices for serving.

# Desserts & Other Fancies

## PINEAPPLE CLOUD DESSERT

8 servings

- ½ cup butter or margarine
- ⅓ cup sugar
- 1 teaspoon vanilla extract
- 1 egg
- 1½ cups all-purpose flour
- ½ teaspoon baking soda
- ½ teaspoon salt
- 1 cup heavy cream
- 1 (12-ounce) can SOLO Pineapple Filling
- 1 cup miniature marshmallows

Preheat oven to 325° F. Cream butter or margarine, sugar, vanilla, and egg together thoroughly. In a separate bowl, sift together flour, baking soda, and salt. Add to creamed mixture, blending well. Spread in bottom of an ungreased 9-inch pie pan. Bake 20 to 25 minutes, or until golden brown. When pie is thoroughly cooled, remove from pan. Cut in half horizontally to make two layers. Whip cream until stiff. Fold pineapple filling and marshmallows into whipped cream. Place one cake layer in pie pan; spread with half of the pineapple mixture. Top with remaining layer and spread remaining pineapple mixture over top. Garnish with chopped walnuts, if desired. Refrigerate at least 3 hours. To serve, cut into pie-shaped wedges.

## LEMON-FILLED CREAM PUFFS

12 large or 16 medium-size puffs

1 cup water
½ cup butter or margarine
¼ teaspoon salt
1 cup all-purpose flour
4 large eggs

1 (12-ounce) can SOLO Lemon
   Filling
1 cup heavy cream
Confectioners sugar

Preheat oven to 400° F. Grease a large baking sheet. In a large sauce-pan, combine water, butter or margarine, and salt. Bring to a boil. Add flour, all at once, and cook over medium heat, stirring constantly, until mixture leaves sides of pan and forms a ball of dough. Remove from heat and add eggs, one at a time, beating well after each addition. Drop spoonfuls of dough, 3 inches apart, onto baking sheet, or squeeze through a pastry tube in desired shapes. Bake 10 minutes. Reduce heat to 350° F. and bake 20 to 25 minutes longer, or until puffs are doubled in size, golden brown, and firm to the touch. Remove from oven and slit side of each puff with a sharp knife to allow steam to escape. Return to turned-off oven and let stand for 10 minutes with oven door open. Cool puffs on wire rack. Whip cream until stiff. Fold in lemon filling. Slit tops off of puffs and fill puffs with mixture. Replace tops, sprinkle with con-fectioners sugar.

**Good Idea: For a filling with a distinctive flavor, try combining 1 (12-ounce) can Solo Prune Filling with ½ cup dairy sour cream. Top cream puffs with a sprinkle of confectioners sugar.**

## STRAWBERRY PARFAIT SQUARES

9 servings

⅔ cup sugar
¼ cup water
1 egg white
1½ teaspoons vanilla extract
1 teaspoon lemon juice

1 cup heavy cream, whipped
1 (12-ounce) can SOLO
   Strawberry Filling
1½ cups graham cracker crumbs

Combine sugar, water, egg white, vanilla, and lemon juice in small mix-ing bowl. Beat with electric mixer at high speed until soft peaks form when beaters are raised, about 3 to 5 minutes. Fold whipped cream into mixture along with strawberry filling and blend until smooth. Sprinkle 1 cup graham cracker crumbs in the bottom of a 9-inch-square baking pan. Spread with filling mixture and top with remaining crumbs. Freeze until firm. To serve, cut into squares.

**Good Idea: This delicious filling can also be poured into an 8-inch baked pie shell or graham cracker crust and frozen. Try this dessert an-other time with any other Solo fruit filling.**

## STRAWBERRY TRIFLE

6 to 8 servings

4 egg yolks
¼ cup sugar
¼ teaspoon salt
1⅔ cups milk
½ teaspoon vanilla extract

1 package ladyfingers
½ (12-ounce) can SOLO Strawberry
 Filling
⅓ cup sweet sherry
1 cup heavy cream

Beat together egg yolks, sugar, and salt. Warm milk over low heat just until bubbles appear around edge. Pour milk slowly into egg mixture, stirring constantly. Return mixture to saucepan and cook over very low heat, stirring constantly, until mixture thickens, or place in top of double boiler and cook over simmering water, stirring, until mixture thickens enough to coat a silver spoon. Remove from heat and cool. Stir in vanilla. Refrigerate until mixture is well chilled. Split ladyfingers in half and fill with strawberry filling. Replace tops. Arrange ladyfingers around edge and bottom of a 1-quart glass casserole or soufflé dish. Pour sherry over ladyfingers and let stand until sherry is absorbed. Spoon chilled custard over ladyfingers. Cover and refrigerate from 1 to 2 hours, until thoroughly chilled. Before serving, whip cream and spread over trifle. Sprinkle almonds on top, if desired.

## LAZY DAY ENGLISH TRIFLE

6 servings

1 (3¾-ounce) package vanilla
 pudding and pie filling mix
6 thick slices pound cake
 (about ½ pound)

1 cup sweet sherry
1 (12-ounce) can SOLO Raspberry
 Filling
½ cup heavy cream

Prepare pudding and pie filling mix according to package directions. Cover and cool. Cut pound cake slices into thick fingers. Place half the fingers in bottom of a glass serving dish. Carefully spoon half the sherry over the fingers. Let stand until sherry is absorbed. Spread half the raspberry filling over the fingers. Pour custard over top of filling. Dip remaining fingers of pound cake in remaining sherry and place on top of custard. Spread top of custard with remaining raspberry filling. Refrigerate until thoroughly chilled. Whip cream until stiff and spread on top of trifle. Refrigerate 30 minutes before serving.


*Opposite: Lazy Day English Trifle, Anchovy Turnovers (page 31),
and Anchovy-Stuffed Mushrooms (page 30)*

## CHEESE BLINTZES

8 to 10 blintzes

| | |
|---|---|
| 3 eggs, well beaten | Butter or margarine |
| 1 cup milk | Cheese Filling (recipe follows) |
| ½ teaspoon salt | Dairy sour cream |
| 2 tablespoons cooking oil | SOLO filling or glaze, any |
| ¾ cup all-purpose flour | desired fruit flavor |

Combine eggs, milk, salt, and oil. Stir in flour and blend well. Let mixture stand about 30 minutes. Heat a scant teaspoon butter or margarine in a 10-inch skillet. Pour in about ¼ cup batter and tilt pan quickly to spread batter over bottom of pan. Cook over medium-high heat until batter sets; bottom should not brown. Turn out onto a platter, stacking cakes bottom side up. When all the pancakes are cooked, divide cheese filling among pancakes, spreading it along one edge of cooked side. Fold sides in and rolled up, starting with side that is spread with filling. Roll tightly and refrigerate at least 1 hour. At serving time, melt 2 tablespoons butter or margarine in a heavy skillet over medium heat. Brown blintzes carefully on both sides, turning once, adding more butter if needed. Serve at once with sour cream and desired filling or glaze.

### Cheese Filling

| | |
|---|---|
| 2 cups pot cheese or dry cottage cheese | ¼ cup sugar |
| 2 eggs, lightly beaten | 2 tablespoons lemon juice |

Combine all ingredients in a small bowl and stir until well blended.

## QUICK TORTONI

12 servings

| | |
|---|---|
| 1 (12-ounce) can SOLO Pineapple Filling | 1 cup SOLO Coconut Flake, lightly toasted |
| ½ (11½-ounce) can SOLO Nut Filling | 1 cup heavy cream, whipped |

Combine fillings and coconut. Fold whipped cream into mixture. Place paper or foil paper baking cups into muffin pan cups. Fill with mixture. Freeze until mixture is firm. Serve in paper cups, garnished with cherries, if desired.

*Opposite: Cheese Blintzes with Cherry Glaze*

## SHREDDED WHEAT CAKES

6 servings

*This is an adaptation of a Greek dessert that requires a special dough called* kataifi, *which resembles shredded coconut.*

6 large shredded wheat biscuits

1 (12-ounce) can SOLO Almond
    Filling or 1 (11½-ounce) can
    SOLO Pecan Filling

¼ cup melted butter or margarine

¼ cup light cream

1 teaspoon cinnamon

½ cup sugar

¼ cup water

2 tablespoons honey

Preheat oven to 350° F. Heavily butter an 8-inch-square baking pan. Hold a biscuit carefully in one hand and, using a very sharp knife, cut through the center of the biscuit, lengthwise. Open biscuit and carefully spread 1/6 of the almond or pecan filling on bottom of biscuit. Close biscuit and place in buttered pan. Repeat process with remaining biscuits. There will be a fair amount of biscuit crumbs that should be put on top of biscuits in pan. Pour melted butter or margarine and cream over top of biscuits. Sprinkle tops of biscuits with cinnamon. Bake 25 to 30 minutes, or until heated through and crunchy on top. During last 5 minutes of baking time, combine sugar and water in a saucepan. Bring to a boil and simmer 5 minutes. Remove from heat and stir in honey. Remove cakes from oven and pour hot syrup over top. Let cool 2 hours before serving.

## SEVEN-LAYER BLUEBERRY DELIGHT

9 servings

*A rich, luscious dessert, not meant for the diet-minded!*

2 cups crushed vanilla wafers

½ cup butter or margarine,
    softened

1½ cups confectioners sugar

2 eggs

1 (12-ounce) can SOLO
    Blueberry Filling

1 (3¾-ounce) package vanilla
    instant pudding

2 cups milk

½ cup finely chopped nuts

1 cup heavy cream or 2 cups
    whipped topping

Sprinkle wafer crumbs on bottom of 9-inch-square pan, reserving ¼ cup for topping. Beat butter or margarine, confectioners sugar, and eggs together with an electric mixer until smooth and well blended. Pour over crumbs in pan. Spread blueberry filling over creamed mixture. Prepare instant pudding according to package directions, using 2 cups milk. Pour over blueberry filling. Add layer of chopped nuts. Whip cream until stiff and spread on top of nuts. Sprinkle with reserved wafer crumbs. Refrigerate 8 hours before serving.

## SOLO DESSERT PIZZA

8 servings

½ cup butter or margarine
⅔ cup brown sugar,
   firmly packed
1¼ cups all-purpose flour
1 cup chopped walnuts
2 (8-ounce) packages
   cream cheese, softened

½ cup granulated sugar
2 eggs
1 cup dairy sour cream
2 teaspoons vanilla extract
2 (12-ounce) cans SOLO filling,
   any desired fruit flavor

Preheat oven to 375° F. Cream butter or margarine and brown sugar together. Add flour and walnuts and blend well. Press dough into a 12- x ⅝-inch round pizza pan, pressing dough up sides. With electric mixer, beat cream cheese and granulated sugar together. Add eggs, sour cream, and vanilla. Beat until smooth. Pour mixture onto crust and spread evenly. Drop filling by spoonfuls on top of creamed mixture, alternating flavors. Bake 30 to 40 minutes. To serve, cut into wedges.

✍ **Good Idea: Use as many leftover fillings as you care to in this recipe for a festive variety of colors and flavors.**

117

## PINEAPPLE BANANA SPLIT DESSERT

14 to 16 servings

2 cups graham cracker crumbs
½ cup butter or margarine,
   melted
½ cup butter or margarine,
   softened
2 cups confectioners sugar
1 egg
1 teaspoon vanilla extract

3 or 4 bananas, sliced
2 (12-ounce) cans SOLO
   Pineapple Filling
1 cup heavy cream or 2 cups
   whipped topping
½ cup chopped nuts
   Maraschino cherries

Combine crumbs and melted butter or margarine. Press mixture firmly on bottom of 13- x 9-inch pan. Refrigerate to chill slightly. Combine softened butter or margarine, confectioners sugar, egg, and vanilla and beat until thick and creamy. Spread evenly over crumb mixture. Place banana slices on top of creamed mixture and top with pineapple filling. Whip cream until stiff and spread over filling. Refrigerate for several hours. To serve, slice into serving portions and top each with chopped nuts and a maraschino cherry.

## CHOCOLATE-ALMOND FONDUE

16 to 18 servings

1 (12-ounce) package chocolate
morsels
2 (1-ounce) squares
unsweetened chocolate
1 (12-ounce) can SOLO Almond
Filling
½ cup heavy cream
2 tablespoons brandy

½ cup SOLO Coconut Flake
Pound cake, cut into large
cubes
Angel food cake, cut into large
cubes
Apple slices
Banana slices

Heat water in bottom part of double boiler. Combine chocolate morsels, unsweetened chocolate, and almond filling in top part of double boiler and cook over hot water, stirring occasionally, until melted and well blended. Stir in cream, brandy, and coconut. If mixture is very stiff, add more cream. Pour mixture into a fondue pot and keep warm over a candle warmer. Place cake cubes and fruit slices on a serving plate. Provide dessert plates and forks or skewers so guests can dip cake or fruit into warm fondue.

118 **Good Idea: Pineapple chunks and pear slices may be added for dipping. Another excellent fruit to serve with this fondue is prunes. To make them really outstanding, pit them and stuff them with any desired flavor Solo filling. The fondue also makes a delicious sauce to serve over ice cream or cake slices.**

## NUTTY NUTS

4 dozen

2 packages refrigerated crescent
rolls (16 rolls)
1 (11½-ounce) can SOLO Nut
Filling

Oil or shortening for
deep-fat frying

Open rolls and place two together to form a square. Seal center seam with fingers and pat dough out into rectangle. Cut each rectangle into eight 2-inch squares. Place ½ teaspoon nut filling in center of each square. Moisten edges and fold over filling, sealing edges well. Pour oil into a small saucepan to a depth of 2 inches. Heat to 375° F. on a candy or frying thermometer. Drop two or three dough balls into hot fat and cook until browned and crisp all around. Serve immediately and, if desired, sprinkle with confectioners sugar, cinnamon sugar, or dip into warm Chocolate Almond Fondue.

*Opposite: Chocolate-Almond Fondue and Nutty Nuts*

## RASPBERRY MOUSSE

about 8 servings

1 cup milk
4 eggs, separated
3 tablespoons sugar
1 tablespoon red maraschino
  cherry syrup (optional)

½ teaspoon vanilla extract
2 (12-ounce) cans SOLO
  Raspberry Filling
2 cups heavy cream

In top part of double boiler, combine milk, lightly beaten egg yolks, and sugar. Cook over hot water, stirring, until the custard coats a spoon. Remove from heat. Blend in cherry syrup and vanilla. Refrigerate until thoroughly chilled. Rub raspberry filling through a wire strainer. Whip cream until stiff. Fold chilled custard and whipped cream into raspberry filling. Beat egg whites until stiff. Fold carefully into raspberry mixture. Turn into a serving bowl and refrigerate at least 4 hours. Garnish with additional whipped cream, if desired, before serving.

Good Idea: When you remove a mixture from over the hot water in a double boiler and wish to cool it in a hurry, fill the bottom of the double boiler with ice water and place the top of the double boiler over it. Stir the mixture often so that it doesn't set faster than you want it to.

## CABINET PUDDING

6 servings

3 cups ½-inch fresh bread cubes
½ cup SOLO Prune Filling
4 eggs
2 cups milk
2 tablespoons sugar
1 teaspoon vanilla extract

Grated peel of 1 orange
1 (12-ounce) can SOLO Strawberry
  Filling
Juice of 1 orange
¼ cup slivered toasted almonds

Preheat oven to 350° F. Combine bread cubes and prune filling. Spoon mixture into 6 heavily buttered 6-ounce custard cups. Combine eggs, milk, sugar, vanilla, and grated orange peel. Pour mixture over bread cube mixture. Set custard cups in a baking pan containing 1 inch hot water. Bake 25 to 30 minutes, or until centers are firm to the touch. Remove custard cups from the water. In a saucepan, combine strawberry filling, orange juice, and almonds. Heat over low heat just until warm. Unmold each pudding and spoon warm sauce over. Serve warm.

## RUSSIAN APPLE PUDDING

6 to 8 servings

6 to 8 large tart apples, peeled, cored, and thinly sliced (2 to 2½ quarts)
½ (10-ounce) jar SOLO Raisin Sauce
¼ cup dry red wine

1½ teaspoons grated orange peel
¼ cup SOLO Almond Filling
½ teaspoon almond extract
2 tablespoons water
Heavy cream

In a large saucepan, combine all ingredients except cream. Cover and cook 3 minutes. Uncover and simmer 8 to 10 minutes, stirring frequently, until apples are tender but not mushy. Cool slightly. Pour into a serving dish and serve warm with heavy pouring cream.

**Good Idea: For a taste-tempting tart apple pie, prepare pastry for a 2-crust pie. Preheat oven to 400° F. Line a 9-inch pie pan with half of the pastry. Pour in apple mixture. Cover with remaining pastry. Crimp edges and cut slits in top of pastry to allow steam to escape. Bake 30 to 40 minutes, or just until crust is well browned. Serve pie warm with whipped cream, if desired.**

121

## SOLO ICE CREAMWICHES

8 servings

1½ cups crisp rice cereal
¼ cup brown sugar, firmly packed
¼ cup butter or margarine, melted
½ cup chopped nuts

1 cup SOLO Coconut Flake
1 to 1½ quarts vanilla ice cream, softened
1 (12-ounce) can SOLO Strawberry Filling

Combine cereal, brown sugar, butter or margarine, nuts, and coconut and mix lightly. Pat half the mixture into a buttered 8-inch-square pan. Spread slightly softened ice cream evenly over the top. Sprinkle with remaining cereal mixture and press down lightly into ice cream. Cover and freeze until serving time. To serve, spread with strawberry filling and cut into squares.

## SOLO SAUCES FOR ICE CREAM OR PUDDINGS

Combine 1 (12-ounce) can Solo Date Filling, 2 tablespoons grated orange peel, and ¼ cup orange juice. Serve over ice cream and top with a few chopped pecans.

Combine 1 (12-ounce) can Solo Apricot Filling and ½ cup marshmallow creme. Serve over sherbet or ice cream and top with a few toasted salted almonds.

Combine 1 (12-ounce) can Solo Almond Filling and ¾ cup chocolate sauce.

Spoon Solo Pineapple Filling over vanilla ice cream and top with toasted Solo Coconut Flake.

Combine 1 (12-ounce) can Solo Prune Filling, 1 tablespoon lemon juice, ¼ cup honey, and ¼ teaspoon cinnamon. Use to top ice cream or warm gingerbread.

Combine ½ (11½-ounce) can Solo Nut Filling and ½ (12-ounce) can Solo Date Filling with ¼ cup dark corn syrup and 3 to 4 tablespoons lemon juice. Stir well and add a pinch of salt.

### APRICOT SAUCE                                                about 2 cups

| | |
|---|---|
| ¼  cup butter or margarine | 1  (12-ounce) can SOLO Apricot |
| 2  tablespoons all-purpose flour |     Filling |
| ¼  cup orange juice | ¼  cup sugar |

Melt butter or margarine in a small saucepan. Stir in flour and cook over low heat 30 seconds. Remove from heat and stir in orange juice. Add apricot filling and stir until mixture is smooth. Cook over medium heat, stirring constantly, until mixture thickens. Remove from heat and stir in sugar. Let mixture cool. Store in the refrigerator and use over cake slices or ice cream.

*Opposite: Solo Sauces for Ice Cream—Apricot-Mallow, Date-Orange, and Cherry Glaze*

## BUTTERSCOTCH ALMOND SAUCE

2½ to 3 cups

¼ cup butter or margarine
1 cup brown sugar, firmly
   packed
½ cup light cream

3 eggs, separated
1 (12-ounce) can SOLO Almond
   Filling

Blend butter or margarine and brown sugar together. Stir in cream and lightly beaten egg yolks. Add almond filling. Place in top part of double boiler and cook over hot water until smooth and thick. Remove from heat. Beat egg whites until stiff but not dry. Fold into almond mixture. Serve hot over sponge or pound cake, nut cake, or ice cream.


## ALMOND RUM SAUCE

about 1½ cups

1 tablespoon cornstarch
1¼ cups water
⅓ cup SOLO Almond Paste
2 tablespoons butter or
   margarine

2 tablespoons dark rum
1 tablespoon sugar
½ teaspoon salt

In a saucepan, combine cornstarch and water. Bring mixture to a boil and cook until clear. Cut up almond paste and add to hot mixture; stir until well blended. Add remaining ingredients and heat until butter or margarine melts and mixture is well blended. Serve either hot or cold over steamed pudding, day-old cake, or ice cream.


## SOLO RICE CREAM

5 to 6 servings

1 cup cooked rice, cooled
1 cup heavy cream, whipped
½ cup miniature or cut-up
   marshmallows

1 (12-ounce) can SOLO Apricot
   or Pineapple Filling
Toasted slivered almonds

Combine all ingredients, except almonds. Spoon into sherbet glasses. Top with almonds and refrigerate to chill before serving.

## STRAWBERRY SOUFFLE

8 to 10 servings

1 (6-ounce) package strawberry-
   flavored gelatin
1½ cups SOLO Strawberry Glaze

1 (3-ounce) envelope whipped
   topping mix

Prepare gelatin according to package directions. Refrigerate until slightly thickened. Beat with a rotary beater until mixture stands in peaks. Fold in strawberry glaze. Prepare topping mix according to package directions. Fold into strawberry mixture. Pour into a 6-cup mold. Refrigerate until firm.

## SOLO SPEEDY TOPPINGS

*For ice cream:* Put warm or chilled Solo Strawberry, Blueberry, Cherry, or Peach Glaze on top of your favorite flavor of ice cream or sherbet. *For cake:* Spread ½ cup Solo Strawberry, Blueberry, Cherry, or Peach Glaze on a slice of pound cake or angel food cake. *For waffles:* Spread warm Solo glaze of your choice over waffles and decorate with whipped topping.

## SOLO MILKSHAKE

2 to 3 servings

1 pint vanilla ice cream
2 cups milk

½ cup SOLO glaze, any desired
   flavor

Combine all ingredients in blender and beat until smooth. Pour into tall chilled glasses and serve immediately.

## MARZIPAN

1½ to 2 dozen

1 (8-ounce) can SOLO Almond
   Paste
¼ cup light corn syrup
1 cup confectioners sugar

⅔ cup marshmallow creme or
   melted marshmallows
Food coloring, any desired
   colors

Cut up almond paste into small pieces. Add corn syrup and confectioners sugar and mix until smooth. Add marshmallow creme and blend well. Divide confection among small bowls and color or tint as desired. Shape into miniature fruits or other desired shapes.

# Index

Listed below are your favorite Solo fillings, glazes, sauces, and special products and the recipes that contain them.

127

**128**